T0391500

MAHASTHAN RECORD REVISITED

The slim monograph *Mahasthan Record Revisited: Querying the Empire from a Regional Perspective* is an excellent example of rigorous historical scholarship. Susmita Basu Majumdar takes a short inscription of which only six lines are available, critically analyses the different interpretations of it, and provides her own reading that differs on certain crucial terminological interpretations. Dismantling the record line by line, Majumdar demonstrates the need to contextualise sources keeping in mind the larger processes at play in a locality, a region, and at the trans-regional level. On the whole, this is a comprehensive coverage in terms of themes that have been picked up, and the manner in which they have been dealt with.

Professor Mahalakshmi
Jawaharlal Nehru University, New Delhi

'A ground-breaking book reassessing history, epigraphy and numismatics; a new vision of Mahasthan-Pundranagara with regional and national perspectives.'

Professor Osmund Bopearachchi
Emeritus Director of the CNRS at the École Normale Supérieure and Adjunct Professor of Central and South Asian Art, Archaeology, and Numismatics, University of California, Berkeley

A small record consisting of six to seven lines that has been published by eminent epigraphists several times, would require a fresh interpretation was almost beyond imagination. It was by chance that the Indian Museum displayed the Mahasthan stone plaque, and after seeing this record, several questions arose which demanded a fresh interpretation, and this enquiry finally culminated into this slim monograph. The book attempts a re-reading of this inscription and also a fresh interpretation. It tries to situate this record in a broader canvas by interrogating the record along with several other evidences. This finally leads us to look at the Mauryan Empire from a regional perspective.

Susmita Basu Majumdar, Professor, Department of Ancient Indian History and Culture, University of Calcutta, specializes in early Indian epigraphy and numismatics. Her research interests also include history of medicine and surgery and history of early Indian religion, especially Ājivikism and Śaivism. Her publications include: *The Mauryas in Karnataka* (Kolkata, 2016) and *Money and Money Matters in Pre-modern South Asia* (co-edited with S.K. Bose, New Delhi, 2019).

Mahasthan Record Revisited

QUERYING THE EMPIRE FROM A REGIONAL PERSPECTIVE

Susmita Basu Majumdar

Routledge
Taylor & Francis Group
LONDON AND NEW YORK

MANOHAR
2023

First published 2023
by Routledge
4 Park Square, Milton Park, Abingdon, Oxon OX14 4RN

and by Routledge
605 Third Avenue, New York, NY 10158

Routledge is an imprint of the Taylor & Francis Group, an informa business

© 2023 Susmita Basu Majumdar and Manohar Publishers

The right of Susmita Basu Majumdar to be identified as the author of the editorial material, and of the authors for their individual chapters, has been asserted in accordance with sections 77 and 78 of the Copyright, Designs and Patents Act 1988.

All rights reserved. No part of this book may be reprinted or reproduced or utilised in any form or by any electronic, mechanical, or other means, now known or hereafter invented, including photocopying and recording, or in any information storage or retrieval system, without permission in writing from the publishers.

Trademark notice: Product or corporate names may be trademarks or registered trademarks, and are used only for identification and explanation without intent to infringe.

Print edition not for sale in South Asia (India, Sri Lanka, Nepal, Bangladesh, Pakistan or Bhutan)

British Library Cataloguing-in-Publication Data
A catalogue record for this book is available from the British Library

ISBN: 9781032520698 (hbk)
ISBN: 9781032520704 (pbk)
ISBN: 9781003405061 (ebk)

DOI: 10.4324/9781003405061

Typeset in Baskerville 12/14
by Ravi Shanker, Delhi 110095

MANOHAR

To

PROFESSOR PATRICK OLIVELLE
Emeritus Professor
University of Texas, Austin

Contents

List of Figures 9

Preface 11

Acknowledgements 15

1. Mahasthan and the Discovery of the Record 19

2. Mahasthan Fragmentary Stone Record Revisited 27

3. Sohgaura Bronze Plaque Contextualized 48

4. More on Granary, Treasury, Grains and Money 58

5. In and Out of Emergency 73

6. The Mahasthan Record Reassessed 78

7. Querying the Empire 87

Select Bibliography 101

Index 109

Colour Plates 113

List of Figures

1.1. Estampage of the Mahasthan record (*Courtesy*: Archaeological Survey of India, Epigraphy Branch, published in *Epigraphia Indica* by D.R. Bhandarkar) 23

1.2. Estampage of the Mahasthan record (*Courtesy*: Archaeological Survey of India, Epigraphy Branch) 24

1.3. Estampage of the Mahasthan record (*Courtesy*: Archaeological Survey of India, Epigraphy Branch) 24

2.1. The Mahasthan record (front side or the incised side) (*Courtesy*: Indian Museum, Kolkata) 29

2.2. The Mahasthan record (reverse side with finely polished) (*Courtesy*: Indian Museum, Kolkata) 29

2.3. The Mahasthan record showing the width of the stone (*Courtesy*: Indian Museum, Kolkata) 30

2.4. The Mahasthan record showing the polished ends and width of the stone (*Courtesy*: Indian Museum, Kolkata) 30
2.5. The Mahasthan record from the side showing the width of the stone (*Courtesy*: Indian Museum, Kolkata) 30
2.6. Jogimara cave inscription, Chhattisgarh (*Courtesy*: Indian Museum, Kolkata) 45
3.1. Sohgaura and other important sites in Bengal and Odisha (*Courtesy*: Ms. Monalisa Rakshit) 49
3.2. Sohgaura bronze plaque inscription (*Courtesy*: Mr. Soumya Ghosh) 50
3.3. Close up of a portion of the Sohgaura inscription showing the Mauryan official symbol and the *dhvajā* inside with the same symbol as depicted in miniature 53
4.1. Imaginary reconstruction of the shape of the Mahasthan record 59
4.2. Close up of the Sohgaura inscription showing the images and symbols depicted on the top of the plaque 60
4.3. Coins from Wari-Bateshwar (*Courtesy*: British Museum, London) 70
4.4. Coins with increased alloy proportion issued from '*anyatra*' or outside the Mauryan territory (*Courtesy*: British Museum, London) 71

Preface

THIS IS an accidental book or a booklet. The fact that a small record consisting of six to seven lines that has been published by eminent epigraphists several times, would require a fresh interpretation was almost beyond imagination. It was by chance that the Indian Museum displayed the Mahasthan stone plaque, and after seeing this record, several questions arose which demanded a fresh interpretation, and this enquiry finally culminated in this slim monograph.

The book does not limit itself to the re-reading of this inscription; the insights thrown up during a series of discussions following the three presentations that I have made in this interim period, have necessitated a fresh interpretation. Never could I imagine a small record like the Mahasthan fragmentary stone inscription could lead us to such significant inferences and conclusions. The initial part of this book discusses the discovery of the record and the environs of Mahasthan. Some of the important readings and interpretations by earlier scholars have been reproduced here for the convenience of readers to compare them, before going through the fresh reading and interpretation put forth by the present author. I have also brought into focus the Sohgaura bronze plaque inscription which is another enigmatic contemporary record. It is engraved on a tiny plaque of bronze, and it is the first inscription on metal which was meant for display. It is almost imperative to mention this record as it is not only contemporaneous but also mentions a similar emergency situation like the Mahasthan record. The discussion on the similarities and dissimilarities between the two records helps us to understand the attitude of the Mauryan state and its capacity to deal with major emergencies, both natural calamities and emergency situations caused due to human agency.

The last four chapters which form the second segment of the book opens with a discussion on granary, treasury, grains and money of the Magadhan Empire, which helps in situating the text and the context of the Mahasthan record. This has led to a reassessment of the record which includes a discussion on the nature of the emergency and its locale. In this context, the book discusses the other archaeological artefacts from Mahasthan, especially the coins and their impact on the interpretation. A proper understanding of the numismatic and the monetary scenario of early Bengal helps to understand the situation at Mahasthan. The final chapter is devoted to a discussion on the relation of Bengal with the Mauryan state or its position in the Mauryan state. The regional perspective is very significant, and it leads to an altogether different paradigm. One may accept it or negate it, but one cannot ignore the sources which speak louder than the voices of the historians. The intention here is just to read the voices, whispers and silences and interrogate the sources for making a fresh interpretation. Hence, the final chapter

'Querying the Empire' attempts to understand the empire from the regional perspective and vice versa.

Colour photographs are reproduced at the end, for the convenience of the readers.

Kolkata SUSMITA BASU MAJUMDAR
August 2022

Acknowledgements

THE AUTHOR is thankful to all the epigraphists who have burnt midnight oil for reading this record. The varied readings and interpretations have led the present author to reinvestigate the record for a fresh interpretation. Thanks to the authorities of the Indian Museum, who on the occasion of International Museum's Week, took the decision of displaying this record for the first time. If I had not seen the record, this interpretation would not have been possible. I am immensely grateful to Dr. Sayan Bhattacharya, Education Officer, Indian Museum, who had provided me with high resolution photographs of the record and also invited me to present my new research in the Indian Museum on the 'Re-reading the Mahasthan Brāhmī Inscription *c.*3rd Century BCE'. I am also thankful to Dr. Satyakam Sen, Indian Museum for his kind help.

I am immensely grateful to three scholars without whose help this book would not have taken shape. I have dedicated this work to Prof. Patrick Olivelle who is not aware of his contribution to the making of this book. I was stuck with a problem of interpreting the term '*su-atyāyika*' in this record. The prefix '*su*' which means 'good' and the term '*atyāyika*' which means 'an emergency' seemed contradictory and I was stuck with the term and the final interpretation of the record depended on the exact interpretation of this term. I was thinking about a good occasion in an emergency situation like marriage or child birth while the people were facing an emergency. It was the intervention of Prof. Ranabir Chakravarti to whom I had sent my interpretation. He had severe objections to this interpretation of the term and mentioned in his email that no emergency could be 'good emergency', as emergency is a negative term. Then I wrote to Patrick (as I call him) and he came to my rescue in the emergency as he mentioned that '*su-atyāyika*' would mean extreme emergency or intense emergency just like '*su-krodha*' means extreme anger and '*su-tapas*' extreme austerity in the same manner '*su-atyāyika*' here may be taken as intense emergency. This became the key to the riddle of solving the Mahasthan puzzle. I am also thankful to Prof. Jagatram Bhattacharyya, Visva-Bharati University, Santiniketan for helping me with cross-checking the Prakrit words and their interpretation. His approval of my interpretation was like a peer reviewer's comment sanctioning a new interpretation. I shall always remain grateful to him for helping me any time with his immense knowledge of Prakrit language.

After the Indian Museum lecture this talk was delivered on two more occasions and these have helped me immensely and the questions that the audience raised led me to think in terms of writing a booklet or a book on this inscription. This could very well have been a long article in a reputed journal but in that case we would have lost the opportunity to add all the readings and interpretations at liberty. I am thankful to Mr. Ramesh Jain for instantly agreeing to publish this small book from their publication house. I am thankful to Dr Sayantani Pal my friend and the present Head of the Department of Ancient Indian History and Culture, University of Calcutta for organizing an occasional lecture on 'Interrogating the Mahasthan Record' on 3 June 2022. This was mainly for those who had missed the Indian Museum lecture, especially keeping the postgraduate students in mind. My heartfelt gratitude to my friend Prof. Mahalakshmi, faculty Jawaharlal Nehru University, New Delhi for organizing a talk entitled 'Earliest Administrative Notification from Bengal: Revisiting the Mahasthan Record' in her department on 15 June 2022. All these talks have helped me to strengthen my arguments and shape them in an articulate manner. I am thankful to each and every person who was present in these talks and raised questions as their questions and suggestions have not only enriched my knowledge but also have helped me to address some of them here.

I am also thankful to Mr Rajib Chakraborty for helping me with graphic designing and making the imaginary shape of the complete plaque as this is a fragmentary stone piece and the reconstruction clearly shows that we have almost lost half of it. This reconstruction would not have been possible without the photographs from the Indian Museum providing the details of the sides reflecting the intact portions and the fragmentary ends of the record.

I am also thankful to Dr Munirathnam Reddy, Director, Epigraphy Branch, Archaeological Survey of India, for being generous enough to provide the three estampages (impressions) of the Mahasthan record from their collection.

I am grateful to my PhD scholars Ms Chandrima Das for helping me with this publication and also Mr Soumya Ghosh for his work on Sohgaura, which was an outcome of my classroom teaching, and his insights led him to a fresh interpretation of this significant record, which I have used here. I would again like to thank Prof. Mahalakshmi for a separate reason all together. Jawaharlal Nehru University lecture had a different orientation and we had been discussing the position of Bengal in the Mauryan empire and it was she who suggested the second portion of the title of this book, i.e. 'Querying the Empire from the Regional Perspective'. I would like to thank Prof. Swadhin Sen, Jahangirnagar University for being so energetic, encouraging and for taking so much interest in the record and my interpretation. Thanks to him for sending material on Wari-Bateshwar which have been very helpful. Finally, my thanks to Ms. Monalisa Rakshit for making the map for this monograph.

SUSMITA BASU MAJUMDAR

1

Mahasthan and the Discovery of the Record

Mahasthan is located 13 km north of Bogra city in Bangladesh, on the banks of river Karatoya in the Barind tract (24°N and 26°N latitudes). The ancient territory was known as Varendra and the people of this region are mentioned in texts as Pauṇḍras. It is the present record from Mahasthan, which forms the central theme of this book, where it is mentioned as Puṇḍranagara, the suffix '*nagara*' denotes that it was an urban centre or a city. It is interesting to note that this city is designated as the city of the Pauṇḍra people. There are two such large archaeological sites which may claim to be urban centres located in the Varendra subregion—one is Mahasthan and the other is Bangarh located between the rivers Atrai and Punarbhava. Bangarh is much smaller in size as far as the settlement archaeology of the site suggests (rampart enclosure 1800′ × 1000′). Out of these two settlements, Mahasthan was more important as the name Puṇḍranagara suggests reflects its huge size (rampart enclosure 5000′ × 4500′). Later this also became the name of the larger territorial unit, i.e. Puṇḍravardhana *bhukti.* The continuity of these two urban centres at least up to the early medieval period suggests that these had sustained for quite a long period of time.

Mahasthan was mentioned for the first time by Francis Buchanan (later known as Francis Hamilton and also as Francis Buchanan-Hamilton) who probably visited Mahasthan sometime between 1810 and 1816 and mentioned it in a single line saying, 'the ruins of Mahasthan are said to be considerable'. This statement of Buchanan raises doubt in our minds whether he actually visited the site or just mentioned it on the basis of what he had heard. However, this passing reference to Mahasthan came up in his work on the Dinajpur district which was published posthumously quite late in 1833. Even after Buchanan's mention, Mahasthan did not receive any attention and later Charles James O'Donnell and E.V. Westmacott in 1875 and H. Beveridge in 1878 respectively travelled through Bogra district and visited Mahasthan. Their reports on the site of Mahasthan are one of the earliest before Alexander Cunningham's declaration made it a prime archaeological site of Bengal and brought it into limelight in 1879. Then for next 50 years there are no evidences of any exploration of Mahasthangarh. P.C. Sen mentions in his monograph that 'Sir Alexander Cunningham visited Mahasthan in 1879 and identified it with the site of Puṇḍravardhana, the capital city of the ancient *bhukti* or province of that name, frequently mentioned in the records of pre-Muslim days.' (Sen 1929: 2). He was the first to identify Mahasthan with Puṇḍravardhana only to be rectified and attested by the discovery of the Mahasthan inscription in 1931 as Puṇḍranagara (Cunningham 2000: 104–77). Though Cunningham collected some antiquities from the site but while describing Mahasthan Cunningham mentions that it was a forested zone and it gained importance with the British for tiger hunting. He also expressed doubts about exploring this place due to its inhospitable there nature. Another infamous element was the presence of a notorious bandit named Mañju. Bogra was famous for banditry and the most famous rebellion was Mañju's in the eighteenth century. The upper inner segment of the rampart is a relatively a new reconstructed and reflects that the inner area of the fort of Mahasthan was used by the bandits as a sheltering cantonment. However, after Cunningham's mention, several local officers both non-historians and archaeologists, took interest in Mahasthan. In 1897 the District Collector Mr. Batavyal visited the site several times and recovered several antiquities. He has left interesting notes about these antiquities. In 1907 a detailed survey of the fort was made by Mr. K.C. Nandi, District Engineer, who had undertaken uncontrolled excavations in search of antiquities. Excavations were carried out in Khodar Pathar Dhanp in trenches which were filled up, followed by the launching of official excavations by the Eastern Circle of the Archaeological Survey at Mahasthan from 1929 onwards. Scholars attempted to reconstruct the historical framework of the urban centre through a survey of literary sources. A local lawyer Mr. Prabhas Chandra Sen, presented a paper on Mahasthan in the Varendra Research Society and later developed it into a monograph and published it as *Mahasthan and its Environs* in 1929. This monograph was second in the series of publications by the Varendra Research Society in which Sen discussed Mahasthan's topography and history which became a major landmark among the scholarly works on Mahasthan. The excavation by the Eastern Circle Archaeological Survey was carried out under the direction of K.N. Dikshit (1929–30 and again in 1934–6) and he selected the portion lying to the east (with the exception of the rampart) for a detailed excavation which included Govinda Bhita, Munir Ghoon and Bairagi Bhita. The excavations were reported in the Annual Reports of the Archaeological Survey of India in 1933, 1937 and 1940. Mahasthan again became the focus and official excavations were again carried out by the Pakistan Department of Archaeology and Museums under the direction of Dr Nazimmudin Ahmed in 1960–7. Reports of these excavations were published in different issues of Pakistan Archaeology and later published in the form of a booklet in 1975. Since 1971, the Department of Archaeology of Bangladesh carried out several excavations and conservation works, however, these still remain unpublished. Finally, the last phase of excavation of the site was conducted continuously for a period of six years as a joint venture wherein Bangladesh collaborated with the French team led by Md. Shafiqul Alam and Jean-François Salles during 1993–9. This Franco-Bangladeshi joint venture was secured through an inter-governmental agreement in 1992. The excavations were not only done in detail and in a highly methodical manner but also two detailed reports were published along with several articles in various journals and books, including the first interim report in 2001 (Alam and Salles 2001) and the second interim report in 2017 (Alam and Salles 2017). These reports are of immense value in understanding the site. Besides these there are two more archaeological reports published by Jean-François Salles (in French) in 2007 and 2015 (Salles 2007; 2015).

Discovery of the Record

The Mahasthan fragmentary record was not discovered during the process of excavation but on 30 November 1931, Baru (Bari) Faqir of Mahasthangarh village found it on a mound close to the place where the excavations were being conducted (Fig. 2.1). Mr. G.C. Chandra, Superintendent, Archaeological Survey of India, Eastern Circle, acquired it from Bari Faqir for the department and sent it to their Calcutta office. Under the orders of the Director General of Archaeology, it was deposited in the Archaeological Section, Indian Museum, Calcutta. Here, three estampages or impressions of the record were prepared. One of them was published by Bhandarkar in the *Epigraphia India*. All the three impressions were preserved in the office of the Archaeological Survey of India, Mysore office (recently shifted to Chennai). Here we have given all the three impressions (see Figs. 1.1 to 1.3).

FIG. 1.1: Estampage of the Mahasthan record

FIG. 1.2: Estampage of the Mahasthan record

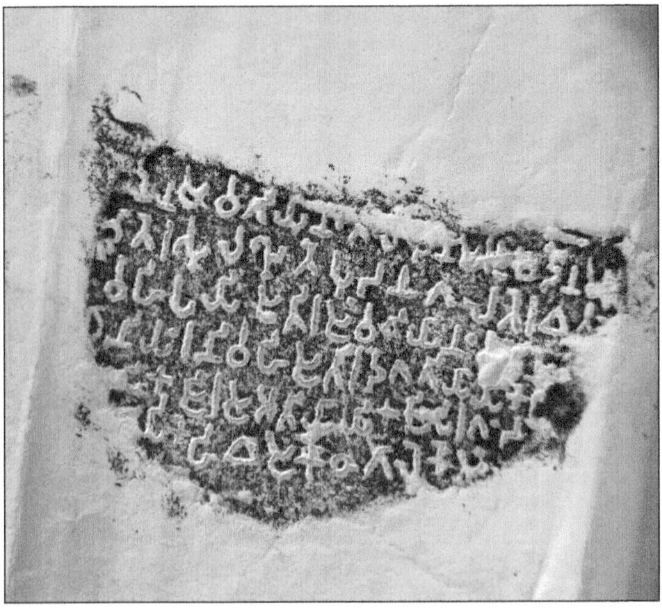

FIG. 1.3: Estampage of the Mahasthan record

Soon after the discovery of the record, a brief account of its content was printed in the columns of a Bengali daily published from Calcutta: *Baṅga Bāṇī*. Government epigraphist Dr. Hiranand Sastri sent an impression to Dr. D.R. Bhandarkar who was in the process of writing an article on the recently discovered inscription. Meanwhile, on Friday, 22 April 1932, it was again published in English in *Liberty*, p. 4. Bhandarkar commented about this published piece in his article in the *Epigraphia Indica* XXI that the article in *Liberty* does not touch upon any important details of this epigraph. Later, the Director General of Archaeology, India, Rai Bahadur Daya Ram Sahni forwarded a photograph of the Mahasthan record to Bhandarkar. Till then he had not seen the original inscription. When the plaque was deposited in the Indian Museum, Bhandarkar was able to inspect it personally.

The Mauryans, who were ruling the Magadhan empire and had their capital in Pāṭaliputra, created two major bases in the east—Mahasthan and Bangarh. The excavators of Mahasthan point out distinctly that no archaeological remains prior to late fourth century BCE have been reported from Mahasthan. As far as the urban centre of Puṇḍranagara was concerned, it was selected and quickly built up, probably as an eastern node cum trading centre. Its proximity to the capital at Pāṭaliputra and also to Rajgir reflects the Mauryan intention of creating eastern control bases. The location of Mahasthan on the bank of river Karatoya, probably made it easily accessible and a well-irrigated zone. Besides, it is also reputed for its high level of agricultural fertility. Hence, it was selected and developed as a regional centre from at least the third-fourth century BCE. Thus the external impetus is distinctly visible in the making of this city. Since the site was built in the third-fourth century BCE, the labour-intensive landscape modifications like a fortification wall, artificial ponds, rice/paddy terraces are distinctly noticeable. There would have been a considerable population at the place to build this fort, its rampart and a moat. Excavations reflect sophisticated agricultural practices at Mahasthan. No archaeological or historical documents suggest any settlement outside the fortified urban core in the early historic period, except Govinda Bhita, which is also not far off from the rampart wall almost located at a distance of 100 m north of the rampart. Though this fortification seems to be the core or the nodal point in the network as suggested by Chattopadhyaya (2003: 70), we may consider it to be the settlement locality and the rest of the areas representing the ancillary settlements which supported this urban centre. The fortification ensured the protection of this urban centre as the region around would have been forested and the term '*sulakhite Puḍanagale*' in the Mahasthan record, which denotes well-protected Puṇḍranagara. This description fits quite well with the fortified city of Mahasthan.

2

Mahasthan Fragmentary Stone Record Revisited

THE MAHASTHAN RECORD was first published by Bhandarkar in 1931–2 and since then several scholars have attempted re-readings, interpretations and explanations of it. The small inscription of which only six lines are extant, was so thought-provoking and controversial that the translations do not match with each other. Moreover, the chronological sequence of reading the texts and attempting its translations also lead us to a very interesting trajectory of how scholars had been engaged with this extremely important document. Even after more than 90 years of its discovery it has not failed to excite us. Here we shall be looking at the readings of different scholars in detail and finally we shall place our re-reading.

I. Mahasthan Fragmentary Stone Inscription

The record is mentioned by Bhandarkar as engraved on a piece of hard limestone. Since then all the scholars have quoted him and no one has it been argued otherwise. Bhandarkar was given this information from the Museum authorities who sent the record to him and neither did he question it nor got it examined by a professional geologist. He does not address issues like is it possible to find out what could be the source of the stone? He also does not provide any photograph of the flip side of the inscription. This makes it a little problematic to imagine whether the stone on which the record was dressed or not. Though the exact size of the record was given as $3\frac{1}{4}'' \times 2\frac{1}{4}'' \times \frac{7}{8}''$ but photographs of the sides of the records were not published, neither does Bhandarkar attach any importance to it.

Here we would like to mention that the stone could also be sandstone.[1] Though the size mentioned by Bhandarkar clearly shows that it was a very small piece of stone yet the clear and bold published inscription image gives a larger impression in mind. The size of the record when seen with the naked eye is extremely small. The reverse or the flip side is finely polished (see Fig. 2.2), thus it was a well-prepared dressed piece of stone. Even the sides of the stone are polished only at one place the polish can be made out (see Figs. 2.3, 2.4 and 2.5). Considering the polished end on the side, an attempt can be made to reconstruct the shape and probable size of the record.[2]

[1]It should be examined and confirmed by a professional geologist. If possible a comment on its place of origin would also be a welcome addition.

[2]This can be done in the same manner as the reconstruction of pottery shapes are done from potshards.

FIG. 2.1: The Mahasthan record (front side or the incised side)

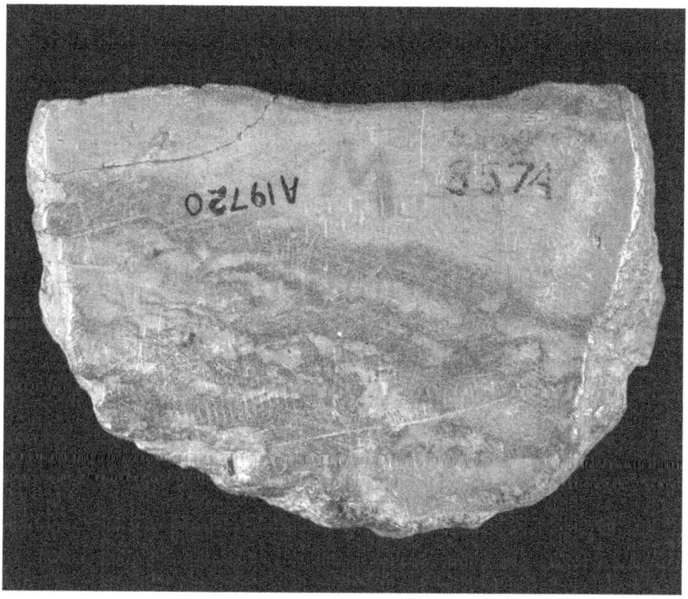

FIG. 2.2: The Mahasthan record
(reverse side with finely polished)

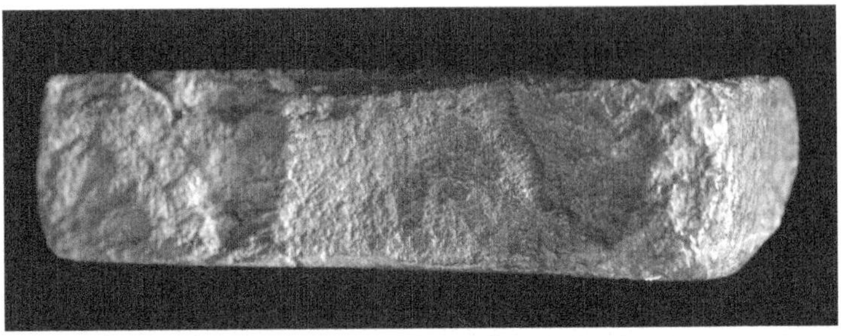

FIG. 2.3: The Mahasthan record
showing the width of the stone

FIG. 2.4: The Mahasthan record
showing the polished ends and width of the stone

FIG. 2.5: The Mahasthan record from the side
showing the width of the stone

We have attempted an imaginary reconstruction which will be discussed later. The probable shape seems to be round or oval.

The language of the record is Prakrit and the dialect is Māgadhī, though certain specific characters of Māgadhī Prakrit like '*sa*' and '*ṣa*' become '*śa*'. This feature is missing and here we find the presence of dental variety only. The script employed to incise is third century BCE or Aśokan Brāhmī.

II. Readings and Interpretations

We shall now discuss each reading and interpretation here and then finally attempt a re-reading.

'Mauryan Brahmi Inscription of Mahasthan': Bhandarkar (1931)[3]

TEXT

Line 1: *nena Sa[ṁ]va[ṁ]gīy[ā]naṁ [Galadanasa] I Dumadina-[mahā]*
Line 2: *māte I sulakhite Puḍanagalate I e[ta]ṁ*
Line 3: *[ni]vahipayisati I Saṁva[ṁ]giyānaṁ [ca di]ne [tathā]*
Line 4: *[dhā]niyaṁ I nivahisati I da[ṁ]g[ā]tiyāy[i]k[e] d[evā]-*
Line 5: *[tiyā][yi]kasi I su-atiyāyika[si] pi I gaṁḍa[kehi]*
Line 6: *[ḍhāni][yi]kehi esa koṭhāgāle kosam [bhara]-*
Line 7: *[ṇīye]*

[3]Bhandarkar does not use diacritical marks in the title of his article but in the content list, the editor has used diacritical marks in the words Brahmi and Mahasthan. However, there should be diacritical marks in Brahmi but since Mahasthan is a modern name, the use of diacritical marks was not required.

TRANSLATION

To Galadana (Galārdana) of the Saṁvaṁgīyas ... (was granted) by order. The Mahāmātra from the highly auspicious Puṇḍranagara will cause it to be carried out. (And likewise) paddy has been granted to the Saṁvaṁgīyas. The outbreak (*of distress*) in the town during (*this*) outburst of superhuman agency will be tied over. When there is an excess of plenty, this granary and the treasury (*may be replenished*) with paddy and *gaṁḍaka* coins (Bhandarkar 1931: 83–91).

DISCUSSION

Here Bhandarkar read Galadana in the first line of the record and took it as a proper name. However, the letter is '*ta*' and not '*ga*'. If considered as '*ga*', the size of the character is almost half the size of the rest of the letters and this inscription is so well constructed and executed that each and every letter is almost equal in size. Hence it can only be read as '*ta*'. He also considered this as an order, i.e. an administrative order. Bhandarkar assumed that the broken portion, which can be read as *māte* in its original form, could be *mahāmātra* and hence this reconstruction. He also took *Saṁvaṁgīyas* as a group and it is he who explained this term as a confederacy of the Vaṅga citing the case of Saṁvṛijjis as a group, or confederacy of the Vṛijjis. Bhandarkar's explanation of emergency was that of a distress caused mainly due to a superhuman agency is quite clear. Further he assumed that this record was a loan document and it refers to a loan to *Saṁvaṁgīyas*, though there is no word to indicate a loan or its replenishment.

The Old Brahmī Inscription of Mahāsthān: Barua (1934)[4]

TEXT AS FOUND INSCRIBED

Line 1: *?(n)ena savagiyānaṃ (talada)na(sa) I dumaṃ dina(sa)*
Line 2: *māte I sulakhite puṃḍanagalate I etaṃ*
Line 3: *(n)ivahipayisati I savagiyānaṃ (ca) ine*
Line 4: *(dh)āniyaṃ I nivahisati I dagatiyāy(i)ke pi (a)-*
Line 5: ... *(y)ikasi I suatiyāyikasi pi I gaṃḍa - - - -*
Line 6: ... *(y)ikehi esa koṭhāgāle kosaṃ- -*
Line 7: - -

TEXT RECONSTRUCTED

Line 1: *[a] nena Savagiyānaṃ t[e]lad[i]nasa dumaṃ dina S[u-*
Line 2: *māte sulakhite Puṃḍanagalate etaṃ*
Line 3: *nivahipayisati [.] Savagiyānaṃ ca [di]ne*
Line 4: *dhāniyaṃ nivahisati [.] Dagatiyāy[i]ke pi a[gi-]*
Line 5: *[tiyā]yikasi suatiyāyikasi pi gaṃḍa[kehi]*
Line 6: *[kākani]yikehi esa koṭhāgāle kosaṃ - -*
Line 7: - - [.]

TRANSLATION

By this [? token], should there be any oil or tree given to the Ṣaḍvargikas [to the person concerned] shall cause that to be conveyed from S[u]mā, Sulakṣmī [and] Puṇḍranagara. [He] shall convey also the paddy given to the Ṣaḍvargikas.

[4]Barua uses diacritical marks for long 'ī' in the case of Brahmī but there seems to be a typographical error, as the long 'ā' vowel marks in Brahmī has been missed in the title. However, throughout the text, the diacritical marks for long 'ā' and long 'ī' have been maintained, which has led us to assume that it was a printing error. Yet, here we have given the title without a long 'ā', following exactly what is there in the printed version.

The treasure-chamber in this storehouse [shall be filled] with *gaṇḍakas* and *kākaṇikas* in emergency due to flood, in emergency due to (fire), also in emergency due to parrots (Barua 1934: 57–66).

DISCUSSION

Barua was of the opinion that *Savagiyānaṃ* mentioned in the text should be taken as a reference to *Ṣaḍvargikas*, a Buddhist community. However, the term can by no means be read as *Ṣaḍvargika*. Since there is a distinct mention of a community which was affected by a calamity, the question that arises here is why the grant was only to be extended to a single Buddhist community? Hence Barua's proposition does not seem convincing. He read *duma* in Prakrit (Sanskrit *druma*) and interpreted it as trees and *tila/tela* as oil, which were according to his interpretation the commodities that were granted to the monks. However, he fails to explain why Buddhist monks would be given trees and oil and not others. It is noteworthy that Barua had recently edited the Sohgaura plaque inscription, another inscription of the same time bracket with a similar theme. This created the misconception that the Mahasthan record also has reference to three place names like the Sohgaura record wherein Mathurā, Cañcu and Medāma are mentioned. Similarly, Barua assumed the mention of S[u]mā, Sulakṣmī [and] Puṇḍranagara in the present record as well. He also assumed that apart from the reference to *gaṇḍakas*, our record also mentions *kākaṇikas* which he considered as copper coins. However, what was correctly interpreted by Barua is the nature of the emergency due to flood but additionally, he assumed two more emergency situations, i.e. emergency due to fire and that due to parrots. He was also at fault when he assumed that the treasure chamber, i.e. *koṣa*, was within the storehouse. The location of a treasury surely cannot be inside a granary.

The Mahāsthān Fragmentary Stone Plaque Inscription: Sircar (1942)

TEXT

Line 1: ... *nena (I) sa[ṁ]vagi(gī?)ya[ā]naṁ [tala dina sa]- I sama dinaI [su]-*
Line 2: *[ma]āte I Sulakhite puḍanagalate I e[ta]ṁ*
Line 3: *[ni]vahipayisati I saṁvagiyānaṁ [ca] [di]ne*
Line 4: *[dhā]niyaṁ I nivahisati I daga-tiyāy[i]ke*
Line 5: ... *[yi]kasi/sua-tiyāyika[si] pi I gaṁḍa[kehi]*
Line 6: ... *[yi]kehi esa koṭhāgāle kosaṁ* ---
Line 7: ---------

TRANSLATION (IN SANSKRIT)

[...mahāmātrāṇāṁ vaca]nena. Ṣaḍvargīyebhyaḥ (yadvā-saṁvargīyebhyaḥ) tilaḥ dattaḥ, sarṣapaṁ (?) [ca] dattam. Sumātraḥ (= tadākhyaḥ puruṣaḥ) sulakṣmītaḥ (= ṛddhimataḥ) Puṇḍranagarataḥ etat, nivāhapiṣyati, Ṣaḍvargīyebhyaḥ ca dattaṁ dhānyaṁ nivakṣyati. [U]dakātyayikāya (= tannivāraṇāya), devātyayikāye (yadvā-agnyātyayikāya), śukātyayikāya [ca] api gaṇḍakaiḥ (mudrābhiḥ) dhānyaiḥ [ca] eṣa koṣṭhāgāraḥ koṣaḥ [ca paripūraṇīyau] II (Sircar 1993: 79–80).

DISCUSSION

Sircar was of the opinion that the order was a verbal one though the tablet or plaque itself is an evidence that the order was a written instruction and vide this token it was to be carried out or executed. Sircar was more or less convinced with Barua's reading yet he mentions both the options. He also read *tila* and took it literally as sesame and then assumed a reference to mustard, however, he also fails to explain why these two commodities were given to combat an emergency. His Sanskrit translation is quite interesting and it reflects a bias towards Barua's interpretation. Bhandarkar, Barua and Sircar all have considered this as a loan and have assumed a word for replenishment at the end. Sircar considers *paripūraṇīyau* to be re-filled or replenished at the end of his Sanskrit translation.

A Epigraphic Document of the Mauryas from Bengal: Bongard-Levin (1958)

TEXT

Line 1: *(a)nena Savagiyānaṃ (tala da) na (sa?) dumaṃ dina (mahā=)*
Line 2: *māte I sulakhite Puḍanagalate I etaṃ*
Line 3: *(ni)vahipayisati I Savagiyānaṃ (ca) (di)ne*
Line 4: *dhāniyaṃ I nivahisati I Dagatiyāy(i)ke pi d(evā)*
Line 5: *(tiyā)(yi)kasi suatiyāyika(si) pi I gaṃda[kehi]*
Line 6: *(dhāni)(yi)kehi eṣa kothāgāle kosaṃ (bhara) (?)*
Line 7: *(?) (ṇīye)*

TRANSLATION

Thereby (by this decree), the sesame and firewood (or timber) shall be available for distribution among the victims. The official-manager from Puṇḍranagara shall see to that. And (this) will save (them). This granary and treasury shall be filled up with grain and coins gaṇḍaka to provide for in the case of flood, famine and all other calamities (Bongard-Levin 1958: 79–84).

DISCUSSION

Bongard-Levin directly considers this document to be a Mauryan record and does not even explain why he has done so as there is absence of any direct Mauryan element in the record. He reads the word Sumātra and takes it as an official designation, however, no such official designation is known to have existed in ancient India. Hence, it is difficult to accept it. He takes the reference to emergency as a general one and any such situation arising out of flood, famine or any other calamities leading to an emergency is to be overcome with the help of this aid.

Mahāsthān Fragmentary Stone Plaque Inscription (Third Century BC): Mukherji and Maity (1967)

TEXT

Line 1: *nena I saṁvagiyānaṁ tala dana sa- I sapa dina I su-*
Line 2: *māte I sulakhite puḍanagalate I etaṁ*
Line 3: *ni * vahipayisati I saṁvagiyānaṁ ca di * ne ***
Line 4: *dhāniyaṁ I nivahisati I daga-tiyā y(i*)ke ***
Line 5: ****yikasi I sua-tiyāyikasi pi I gaṁḍakehi **
Line 6: ****yikehi esa koṭhāgāle kosaṁ ****
Line 7: ****

TRANSLATION

To Gobardhana of the Saṁvaṁgīyas was granted by order (or to the Saṁvaṁgīyas was given by order, sesamum and mustard seeds). The Sumātra will cause it to be carried out from the prosperous city of Puṇḍranagara. (And likewise) will cause paddy to be granted to the Saṁvaṁgīyas. In order to tide over the outbreak of distress caused by flood (or fire, or any superhuman agency) and insects (lit. parrots) in the city, this granary and treasury will have to be replenished with paddy and gaṇḍaka coins (Mukherji and Maity 1967: 39–40).

DISCUSSION

Mukherji and Maity took Bhandarkar's version of Galadana and revised it to Gobardhana, however, this word can clearly be read as '*taladana*' on the record. Then they have taken the cue from Barua and have assumed that *tila*, i.e. sesame seeds and mustard seeds were given. There is no reference to sesame seeds or mustard seeds in the record. They have added the *su* in line 1 next to *māte* in line 2 directly, but this being a fragmentary record there should be a letter after *su* and moreover there is no administrative post as *sumāta*. Hence, this is a faulty assumption. Next they follow Bhandarkar and mention that paddy was to be granted to the *Saṁvaṁgīyas* by this order. However, the reason for the grant has again been assumed as multiple without any reference to the outbreak of distress caused by flood (or fire, or superhuman agency) and *suatyāyika* has been taken as *suka-tyāyika*, i.e. emergency caused due to parrots but they mention it as outbreak of distress due to insects. It is difficult to accept this because if there was flood, then the grains would have been destroyed and there would be no scope for parrots or insects to destroy the grains any further. Again, without any word for replenishment or loan they have assumed that the granary and treasury will have to be replenished with paddy and *gaṇḍaka* coins.

Mahasthan Fragmentary Stone Inscription Revisited

TEXT: RE-READING

Line 1: ....

Line 2: *nena sa[ṁ] vagi(gī?)ya[ā]naṁ taladinasa I dumadinasa*

Line 3: *[mahā]māte I sulakhite puḍanagalate I e[ta]ṁ*

Line 4: *[ni]vahipayisati I saṁvagiyānaṁ [sasa]ne [dinā]*

Line 5: *[dhā]niyaṁ I nivahisati I daga-tiyā[i]yake p[īḍa]*

Line 6: *[yi]kasi I su-atiyāyika[si] pi I gaṁḍa[kehi] I [uvasana/dinā]*

Line 7: *[dhāni]yikehi esa koṭhāgāle kosaṁ [gaṁḍakehi]*

TEXT IN CONTEXT

Line 1: Lost, though the record may also have two lines prior to the present incised portion extant on the fragmentary stone. Scholars unanimously agree that the present line 1 is not the first line of the record and there was a line 1 which we have lost. Hence, line 2 here is line 1 of the readable portion.

Line 2: As the record is fragmentary, the first word is incomplete and only '*nena*' can be read. Probably it stood for '*vacanena*', i.e. by the verbal order (of the King/*Mahāmātra*?) or '*anena*', i.e. vide this token (issued) for Taladina (name of a person[5]) of the *Saṁvangīyas* locality or *Saṁvaṁgīya* (issued

[5]We have taken Taladina and Dumadina as personal names as the medial vowel '*i*' is very distinct and cannot be assumed as *tiladāna* and so on. Taladina and Dumadina were names of persons like Devadina in Jogimara cave inscription with *dina* name ending. Sircar mentions that *dina* is for *datta*, i.e. Devadina is the same as Devadatta.

by *mahāmātra* or an officer named Dumadina *mahāmātra*(?).

Line 3: Dumadina has been mentioned as a *mahāmātra* (?) as this line begins with '*māte*', which is a continuation of *mahāmāte*. It further mentions that it was (issued) from well protected Puṇḍranagara, (*sulakhite Puḍanagalate*, i.e. *surakṣita* Puṇḍranagara where there are no signs of calamity/emergency).

Line 4: mentions '*[ni]vahipayisati I saṁvagiyānaṁ [ca] [di] ne/sasane*' which indicates that it is to be carried or taken (at their own cost which means not to be sent by the authorities at their cost, from Puṇḍranagara) by *Saṁvaṁgīyas/Saṁvargīyas* if sasane is read in place of dine then it stands for 'given paddy vide this order'. The term for paddy comes in the next line.

Line 5: mentions that '*[dhā]niyaṁ*', i.e. paddy is given. Then again the term '*nivahisati*', i.e. take (from a specified store). Then comes the actual reason for which this aid has been given or relief provided. It is '*daga-tiyā[i]yake*', i.e. an emergency situation arising due to water, i.e. flood (*daka>daga* meaning water).

Line 6: mentions '*su-atiyāyika[si] pi/gaṁḍa[kehi]*', '*su-atiyāyika*' refers to a good emergency or a good occasion or ceremony like marriage or any other social event. Thus it mentions that for the emergency arising out of the flood situation or any other genuine emergencies, copper coins, i.e. financial aid, probably on loan is also given from a specific treasury, i.e. '*koṣa*' (this word is probably broken).

Line 7: This line begins with '*yikehi*' then follow the words '*esa koṭhāgāle kosaṁ*'. Thus, at the end after the mention of the store house (*koṭhāgāle*) there is a mention of the term '*kosaṁ*', which stands for treasury. Either at the end of this line or preferably at the end of line 4, we assume that there was a word indicating given or bestowed. The same way in which previous scholars have assumed the probability of the term *bharaniye* at the end in the same manner we have also assumed that there would have been a term for given, i.e. vide this order unhusked paddy and financial aid is bestowed on the *Saṁvaṁgīyas*. The reason for assuming its probable mention in line 6 is that all the lines have 16–17 characters (see Table 1) and it is line 6 where we have 15 characters and moreover its insertion in line 6 towards the end makes perfect sense. Bhandarkar inserted the word '*bharaṇīye*' as a reconstruction after '*kosaṁ*' for indicating that the inscription intended to communicate to the *Saṁvaṁgīyas* that they have to replenish the granary and the treasury. Sircar in the Sanskrit translation mentions '*paripūrṇīyau*' to indicate that this loan is a replenishment.

TABLE 1

Line no.	*No. of letters*	*No. of daṇḍas*
1	Broken/Absent	
2	18	2
3	16	2
4	15 + ?	1
5	16	2
6	14	2
7	14 + ?	0

TRANSLATION

Vide this token *mahāmātra* Dumadina stationed at safe (*sulakhite*, i.e. *surakṣita*) Puṇḍranagara (is notified that) Taladina of the *Saṁvaṁgīya* locality (has to make arrangements) for paddy or unhusked rice (which is granted vide this order) to be carried or taken (at their own cost which means not to be sent by the authorities at their cost from Puṇḍranagara). Take (from specified store). (As there is an) emergency situation due to water, i.e. flood. Unhusked rice (for sowing) and in addition to this those who are facing severe or extreme emergency (for them financial aid, i.e.) copper coins from the treasury (are given or bestowed upon).

One may now read it as an instruction given (vide this order if read *anena*) from the regional centre that paddy (*dhāniyikehi*) is to be taken from this storehouse (where this record or notification was sent). In that case we may assume that a similar record was also sent to the treasury from which the money, i.e. copper coins were to be given to those affected. However, this being a fragmentary record, the details of this treasury are lost. One can see that there was a line 7 in the record but it is completely lost now. There is no word in the record to indicate replenishing the treasury or storehouse though the context of the record leads to an assumption that the aid both in the form of grains and money were extended probably as a loan. Thus, the people of *Saṁvagīyas* (*Saṁvaṁgīyas*) faced an emergency which arose due to water (probably flood) for which this aid both in cash and kind was extended to them to combat the calamity.

Thus, the original purport of the record is to state that by the order of the *Mahāmātra* named Dumadina addressed to a person or official named Taladina of

Saṁvagīya locality, it is stated that a government aid is sent in the form of paddy and financial aid. This stone document thus is a notification recording an official order to the storehouse at Puṇḍranagara. A similar order was also sent to *koṣa*, i.e. treasury (not discovered yet and details also lost). As one cannot expect that the storehouse for storage and distribution of grains and treasury will be located at the same place. Thus, this is a measure taken by the authorities post-flood to combat the disaster or the aftermath of flood. The aid sent in the form of paddy was probably to be used for sowing in the field, in other words for facilitating harvest. The people of *Saṁvaṅgīya* locality who were in severe financial distress were instructed to take money from the treasury. This was probably a loan to be repaid as it mentions two kinds of emergencies—*dagatiyāyika* and *suatiyāyika*. Since there was an emergency and aid was sent to combat it, they were expected to specify their need or type of emergency while taking grains or financial aid from the local office. Farmers would require paddy for sowing in their fields hence paddy was given and in case of severe emergency, one could specify the difficulty and seek financial aid, then one could specify and avail financial aid which would probably have been a loan. *Suatiyāyika* cannot be taken as *sukatiyāyika* or an emergency due to parrots as the record already specifies an emergency arising out of flood. Hence, the agricultural produce would have been affected and in that case parrots cannot damage the harvest; such a reading and interpretation would make it self-contradictory.

Who were the *Saṁvaṅgīyas* in Our Record?

Bhandarkar has given an extremely important and pertinent explanation about the term *Saṁvaṅgīyas*. As we have already discussed, Barua's explanation of *Saṁvaṅgīyas* as Ṣaḍvargika monks of the Buddhist community does not hold ground. Here Bhandarkar gives a similar example of the Vṛjjis and as the term *Saṁvajji* signifies confederacy of the Vṛjjis in the same manner the term *Saṁvaṅgīyas* may also be explained. If this is considered, then this is the earliest reference to the confederacy of the Vaṅgas or a cluster of localities of the Vaṅgas. The ancient territory of Vaṅga comprised the present day areas of Dhaka, Faridpur, Vikrampur and neighbouring regions.

If this was an order to the *Saṁvaṅgīyas* then the question which arises here is why is it found in Puṇḍranagara or Varendra? The record is self-explanatory as it clearly mentions '*esa koṭhāgāle*', i.e. this granary. Hence, the granary located at the well-protected city of Puṇḍranagara was ordered probably by the metropolitan Magadhan authority to send aid to the neighbouring region of Vaṅga which was facing an emergency situation. Vaṅga is a land of rivers and a flood prone zone. At the same time, it was also an agriculturally rich zone, like Varendra. The authorities were looking into the prospect of the next harvest as the floods would have affected the storage of grains in the Vaṅga locality and the winter harvest which takes place during December and January would be affected for want of unhusked paddy for sowing. This also explains that our record is not an immediate aid just after the floods and hence it becomes clear why in place of rice or other food items, unhusked paddy was being provided through this record. One of the major urban centres of Vaṅga was Wari-Bateshwar. Probably, the aid was sent to the *mahāmātra* stationed at this urban centre. We shall discuss this later.

Note on *Daṇḍas* or Full Stops in Our Record and its Implication

Incidentally, the use of the *daṇḍa* (I) to separate words and phrases in this record is noteworthy and is of immense significance. Sircar and Bhandarkar are of the opinion that the punctuation marks or *daṇḍas* used in the record are useless and their futile character has been stressed upon by citing the example of Aśoka's Kalsi inscription where such stops have been used. However, the present author in a recent article (Basu Majumdar et al. 2020: 73–97) has shown elsewhere that these are not useless or futile but were oration marks put by the orator and the copy from which the edict was engraved was the orator's manuscript. Moreover, use of such *daṇḍas* are also found in the contemporary records like the Jogimara cave inscription (Majumdar and Bajpai 2014: 26–37) from Chhattisgarh (see Fig. 2.6). Here too the *daṇḍas* actually

FIG. 2.6: Jogimara cave inscription, Chhattisgarh

help us to understand the exact purport of the record. After the mention of the name of Śutanuka, there is a full stop. Then after the end of the second line there is a full stop after the mention of rock cut bed, i.e. *luna śeye*. Finally, there is a full stop after the mention of Devadina's name (*devadina nama* as it is also suggested by some scholars that there is no use of long vowels and hence *nāma* is mentioned as *nama* here). Then again between this full stop and another one, Devadina has been mentioned as an architect, i.e. *lupadakhe* or *rūpadakṣaḥ*.

In the case of the Mahasthan Fragmentary Stone inscription the full stops are of similar character and they help us to understand the record. These full stops indicate the end of the previous context and the beginning of a new one. When our record is read with the *daṇḍas* as punctuation marks to end the context and begin a new sentence, it makes proper sense.

Line 1: ....
Line 2: *...nena sa[ṁ] vagi(gī?)ya[ā]naṁ taladinasa I dumadinasa*
Line 3: *[mahā]māte I sulakhite puḍanagalate I e[ta]ṁ*
Line 4: *[ni]vahipayisati I saṁvagiyānaṁ[sasa]ne*
Line 5: *[dhā]niyaṁ I nivahisati I daga-tiyā[i]yake p[īḍa]*
Line 6: *[yi]kasi I su-atiyāyika[si] pi I gaṁḍa[kehi]*
Line 7: *[dhāni]yikehi esa koṭhāgāle kosaṁ [gaṁḍakehi]*

The first one can be noticed after the name of Taladina, which reflects that Taladina is an officer of Saṁvaṅgīyas and not Puṇḍranagara. The next full stop follows after the mention of the name Dumadina, who is mentioned as (*mahā*)*mātra*. This is to segregate his identity along with the designation. Then again after *surakṣita* Puṇḍranagara comes the next *daṇḍa* (I) which again marks the end of this context that Puṇḍranagara is well protected. The next *daṇḍa* also comes after two words—*e[ta]ṁ [ni]vahipayisati*—to be taken or carried from here and the context ends here as it is a clear order given to the Saṁvaṅgīyas. Then the following full stop is at the end of the context of unhusked paddy (*[dhā]niyaṁ*) being given to the Saṁvaṅgīyas. After this follows the most instructive order, i.e. 'Take' (*nivahisati*) as the paddy is given now following the order to take it. Then again between the two full stops is another information, i.e. the grant is for those who have suffered due to water (flood). Finally, after this the change of context occurs and between the full stops we find (*su-atiyāyika[si] pi*), i.e. those who have suffered extreme emergencies for them, then follows the next context, i.e. financial aid is provided from the treasury. Hence, while interpreting we have to take all these *daṇḍas* into consideration.

3

Sohgaura Bronze Plaque Contextualized

SOHGAURA IS a small village in the Gorakhpur district of Uttar Pradesh (see Fig. 3.1). The Sohgaura bronze plaque inscription and the Mahasthan fragmentary stone inscription from Bogra district, Bangladesh, moreorless belong to the same time bracket, i.e. *c.*third century BCE. Palaeography of both these records indicate their dating close to the Aśokan records. Besides this these two records are also thematically connected as both are related to calamity and relief measures. The Sohgaura record portrays a pre-calamity situation whereas the Mahasthan inscription records post-calamity relief-management. Though these calamities or emergency situations were not connected to each other, yet both were locality-centric or community-centric calamities. Such calamities leave an impact on the community as a whole. They not only cause damage to human lives, animals and wildlife, nature, environment and ecology but also affect normal social life and may have their impact on material property and

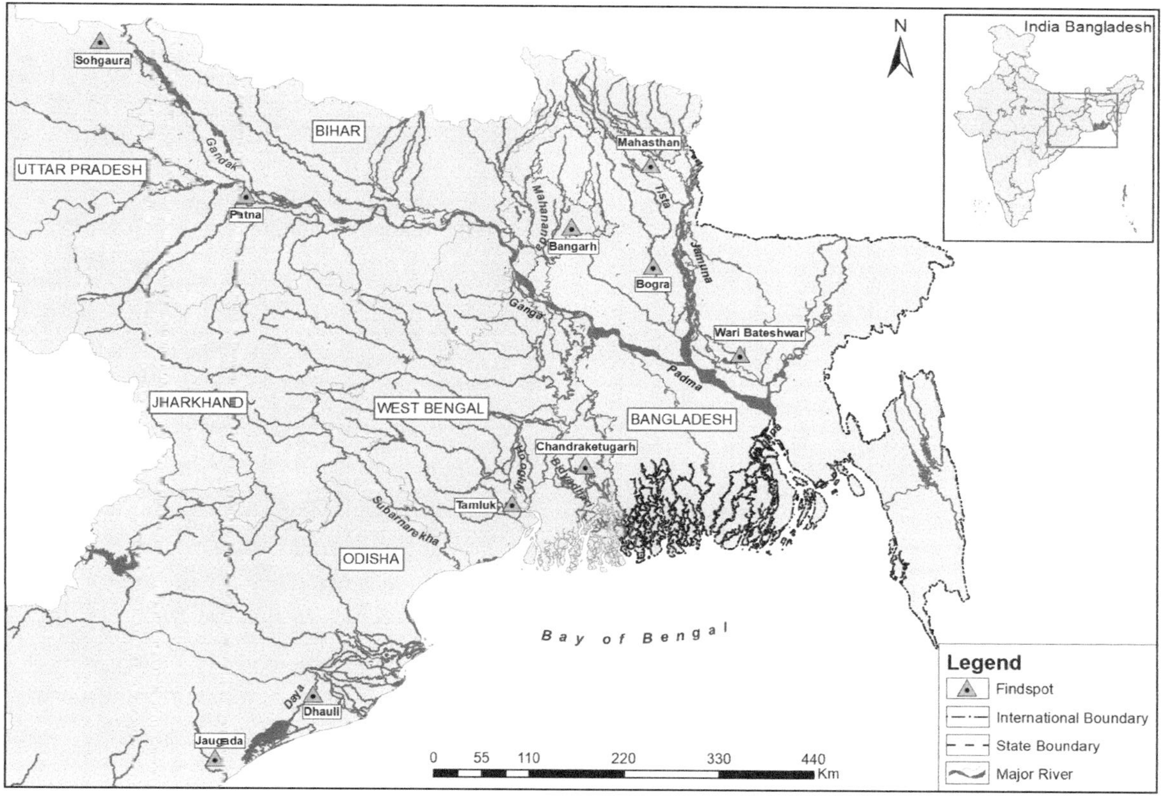

FIG. 3.1: Sohgaura and other important sites in Bengal and Odisha

economy. Here these two records have been revisited and an attempt has been made to critically evaluate them.

Of the two selected epigraphs, the Sohgaura bronze plaque inscription records the administrative order stating the preparatory position of the political authority, if a disaster were to hit the locality (see Fig. 3.2). The question which arises here is that were they apprehending a calamity? Is it failure of monsoon which would have led to the apprehension of the onset of a drought and resultant famine? Is it the apprehension which led to this preparatory position or the issuance of the order to combat a forthcoming disaster situation? A detailed study and analysis of the record is what may lead us to the real purport of the record.

The plaque was an order in the form of a notice which was to be nailed on the door of the granary which was created to store grains and other objects to be taken

FIG. 3.2: Sohgaura bronze plaque inscription

or consumed only in case of an emergency. Besides the Brāhmī inscription, the epigraph also has a few symbols on the top where two granaries have been depicted and the record also mentions two granaries. The inscription has been edited and commented by scholars like Smith and Hoernle (1894: 84–6); Bühler (1896: 265); Fleet (1907: 509–33); Grierson (1907: 683–5); Barua (1930: 32–48); Jayaswal (1938: 1–3); Chakravarti (1941: 203–5); Sircar (1952: 1–3; 2007: 101–3); and Ghosh (2007: 110–13; 2016: 128–38; 2018: 145–52).

Sohgaura Bronze Plaque

TEXT

Line 1: *save ti-yāna mahamagana sasane [I] manavasi tike*[1] *[I]*
Line 2: *dasilimāte usagame vā ete duve Koṭha(ā)gālani*
Line 3: *tighavani mothula-cacu-medāma bhalakana(m) [I] va-*
Line 4: *la kayiyati atiyāyikaya [I] no gahitavaya [II]*

TEXT IN CONTEXT

Notice that all the three (types of) vehicles plying on the highway meet at the three-way junction of Manavasi. The two storehouses (which are) three-tiered (located) at Dasilimāta and Uṣāgrāma are for the load-bearing (vehicles) coming from Mathurā, Cañcu and Medāma (to store their goods). (The goods stored here) may be taken/ consumed by many (for community usage) in emergency situations. Not to be taken (at normal conditions by anyone).

It is evident from the use of '*la*' in place of '*ra*' and other features of the dialect that the record was issued

[1]The letter '*ke*' is very small and has been cramped and accommodated here to form a complete word, i.e. *manavasitike*.

in Māgadhī Prakrit which indicates that it was a royal order from the centre or metropolitan zone of Magadha to the regional centre near Manavasi or Sohgaura. Ghosh who has re-edited the record, draws our attention to the fact that it is an order (*śāsana*) in the form of a notice for all vehicles carrying goods on the highway, i.e. *mahāmārga* meeting at the three-road junction (*tika* > *trika*) at Manavasi (Fleet 1907: 519; Ghosh 2016: 128–38, 2018: 145–52). The place, i.e. Manavasi where roads from three directions, i.e. Mathurā, Cañcu and Medāma, met has rightly been mentioned as a *trika* here. The record mentions two storehouses which were three-tiered (*tighavani* or *trigarbhāni*) where the goods were to be stored. The symbolic representation above the inscribed space in the record clearly depicts two three-tiered storehouses. The official tone of the order of our record is very clear in the short sentences which are mostly instructive like 'for the masses or to be used by the community in emergency situation' (*vala kayiyati atiyāyikaya*)[2] or 'not to be taken' (*no gahitavaya*). There is a depiction of a pillar or post in the top portion of the record. On the top of the pillar is a leaf-like capital and in the centre there is a symbol which may be identified as an official Mauryan symbol, i.e. three-peaked hill with a crescent. This indicates beyond doubt that this was an official Mauryan record (see Fig. 3.3).

Thus the record under discussion mentions that if an emergency situation arises, then goods or required goods may be taken from the two storehouses by those who are affected or the community that is facing the emergency situation. The goods stored in these two storehouses

[2]Ghosh draws our attention to the fact that '*vala*' here means 'to take something' and '*kayiyati*' stands for 'a work to be done by many' indicating the community or masses. *Atiyāyikaya* is an emergency situation.

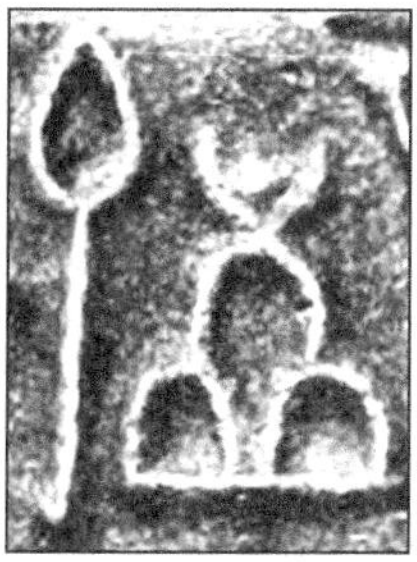

FIG. 3.3: Close up of a portion of the Sohgaura inscription showing the Mauryan official symbol and the *dhvajā* inside with the same symbol as depicted in miniature

were only for emergency situations and were not to be used otherwise is indicated by the use of the phrase '*no gahitavaya*', i.e. not to be taken. The notification was for specific vendors, i.e. only those coming from Mathurā, Cañcu and Medāma to Manavasi. Ghosh assumes that three copies of this record were created—two were probably for the display on the doors of the two store-houses, i.e. at Dasilimāta and Uṣāgrāma, where the store-houses were located, and the third one was probably retained at the administrative office. He further rightly mentions that the size of the plaque was too small to be noticed if displayed at the highway or on a pillar, but if there was a fourth copy then it could have been displayed at the Manavasi junction. At the Manavasi junction one would expect the presence of a big gate or a custom house and a pillar with a flag either facing east or north.[3] One may assume the presence of a *paṇyādhyakṣa* at this regional centre who would have looked into the matter of trading in commodities, controlling prices by storing them during the times of abundance and releasing them during

[3]As the *Arthaśāstra* (2.21.1) mentions, 'the collector of customs and tolls should establish the custom house and a flag facing the east or the north in the vicinity of the big gates' (Kangle 1963: 141).

the times of scarcity.[4] The Sohgaura record reflects the preparatory position of the central administrative office at Magadha which had taken measures to combat a forthcoming famine situation in and around Sohgaura.

In this context one must consider the mention of Cañcu as the name of a famine in the *Meṇḍakāvadāna*. The latter being a late text cannot, however, be taken as a direct evidence and the present author is well aware of the fact that it has no direct connection but we may assume that the intensity of the calamity at Cañcu was massive. To combat such an emergency situation, adequate steps were taken and arrangements were done by the Mauryan metropolitan centre.[5] The calamity probably initiated from Cañcu and was so grave that it was called Cañcu.

Mahasthan and Sohgaura

When the Mahasthan fragmentary record and the Sohgaura bronze plaque are taken together certain things become pronounced. If we consider the Sohgaura record as a plaque then we should also consider the Mahasthan inscription as a plaque as the nature of both the records are similar. One is before the onset of a calamity and the other is a record issued after the calamity. In both the records, the issuing authority cannot be identified on the record. Especially in the case of Sohgaura which is intact we can read the complete text. We are very sure that it does not mention any issuing authority. It is in the form of a government order or an administrative order. In case

[4]*Arthaśāstra* (4.2.32) mentions that, 'in case of damage to the commodities (of traders), he (*paṇyādhyakṣa*) should show them favour from glut of commodities' (Kangle 1963: 261).

[5]As the record is in Māgadhī Prakrit.

of the fragmentary Mahasthan record, the fragmentary nature of the record does not allow us to conclude that it did not mention the issuing authority. However, it is unique as it bears the names of two officials who were involved in the process of disbursement of paddy in the time of calamity. Usually in the Mauryan records we do not find the name of any official. Mahasthan record is an exception. It is an inscribed portable notification for execution which was not meant for display, whereas, the Sohgaura bronze plaque is an inscribed portable notice not for execution with immediate effect but specifically for display on the door of the granary in anticipation of an emergency.

Assessing the Nature of the Mahasthan Record

The question which arises here is that is it a loan document or an official relief measure document? If it were a loan document then there should be a word for replenishment. But our record is fragmentary in nature and hence the word for replenishment may have been broken or lost. But in all probablility if it would have been a loan document, but in that case the time for refund or return of the loan amount would have been specified. Even the interest rate should be mentioned/or if it was interest-free loan, should have been specified in the record. However, our record does not mention any of these. Though it is fragmentary, there is not enough space in the record to assume that all these elements would have been mentioned here.

Another question that arises here is that if the grant was extended to the Saṁvaṅgīyas, then this relief measure was not for immediate relief. If it were so then they should have given edible rice for immediate consumption. Why was unhusked paddy given? The government or local administration was concerned about the revenue that would be generated from the agricultural produce. The record mentions relief in the form of unhusked paddy and financial aid in the form of copper coins.

Money was not given for mass distribution. The *gaṇḍakas* were in all likelihood local currency circulating in the Vaṅga territory and were probably uninscribed cast copper coins. What is interesting to note is that here in this record financial aid was only sanctioned for those facing excessive emergency situation (*su-atiyāyika*), i.e. only in case of grave emergency money was to be released from the official treasury.

This brings us to another issue: who will make an assessment of the intensity of emergency and the requirement of the individual seeking aid? In that case, we will have to assume that vide this government order, sanction of money was made for such a purpose and there would have been an elaborate communication mentioning the amount sanctioned from the government and terms and conditions applicable. It would also have been specified which treasury, i.e. located at which place, was supposed to disburse the aid to the masses, which official was in-charge of the disbursement and how would he assess and disburse the amount to those facing dire necessity.

Here, we would like to assume that if there was a *mahāmātra* stationed at Puṇḍranagara, he might be the one in-charge of the Varendra subregion and similarly there would have been another one at Vaṅga, or any local level officer in-charge of the Saṁvaṅgīyas would have been given the charge of disbursement of the financial aid and its management. Since this involved handling of money, the Mahasthan record mentions both the *mahāmātras* by their personal names. Since this was an administrative record, the individuals Taladina and Dumadina would have to shoulder the responsibility of any dispute as well which would arise in future. This also explains why the Sohgaura bronze plaque inscription does not mention any names. As it is a notification to be put up on the doors of the granary for grains to be stored there for a forthcoming emergency, no officer was addressed. Whereas, in the case of the Mahasthan record, the temporary nature of the emergency needed immediate handling and disbursement of grains and money as aid, hence persons in-charge of handling this temporary situation were named as they were responsible for its execution.

4

More on Granary, Treasury, Grains and Money

THE MAHASTHAN RECORD is fragmentary and is almost semi-circular in shape. There is a possibility that it was round in shape or elliptical. In that case if we consider that there would have been two more lines or one line above line 1 of the present record, then a considerable space remains vacant and it is likely that it might also have a visual illustration on the top, like the Sohgaura record. We have attempted a conjectural reconstruction of the Mahasthan record. As already mentioned, the method applied to reconstruct the shape of potteries, based on pot shards, applying a similar method we have reconstructed this imaginary plaque (the inscribed portion is a meaningless copy of the lines below) (see Fig. 4.1).

FIG. 4.1: Imaginary reconstruction of the shape of the Mahasthan record

Granaries at Sohgaura

The Sohgaura bronze plaque refers to the presence of two granaries at Manavasi junction. It is interesting to note that the record has the depiction of two granaries which are three-tiered structures; however, it is also mentioned in the record that these two granaries were three-tiered (*trigarbhāni*). To differentiate them visually, one granary

FIG. 4.2: Close up of the Sohgaura inscription showing the images and symbols depicted on top of the plaque

has been depicted with a tree in railing with leaves and the other without leaves (see Fig. 4.2). The granary at Manavasi, i.e. Sohgaura, was specifically for storage of grains in anticipation of an emergency. As we have already discussed that this region was struck by a major calamity or disaster named Cañcu which gave the name to the famine. Is it the anticipation of this famine which arose out of drought or low rains and inadequate harvest that the government was gradually getting prepared for aid to the famine-affected people in and around Sohgaura?

On the basis of this, we have also assumed that the Mahasthan record could also be embellished with visual representation of a *koṣṭhāgāra* and a *koṣa* or only a granary, as it was an order in all probability to the granary in-charge at Puṇḍranagara. It may be said with certainty that the record had one line above the present line 1. But this may be extended at most to two lines and in that case a considerable space would be available which might have borne the depiction of the granary. However, this is purely a conjecture.

The presence of a granary as a public building to store grains as revenue or during emergency is a typical feature of an urban centre. Puṇḍranagara which is mentioned as well protected in our record (*sulakhita*, i.e. *surakṣita*) and this is reflected from the presence of a fort, rampart and it also had a granary for emergency purposes.

Treasury

In the Mahasthan fragmentary record, the term used for indicating a treasury is *koṣa*. It is but obvious that the granary and treasury were two separate structures. The *koṣa* or treasury was probably located in Vaṅga as the territory of Varendra, which was a separate locality, would not send financial aid to the territory of Vaṅga. As far as paddy as aid was concerned, one can assume that flood in Vaṅga might have destroyed the stored paddy and hence aid was extended from Varendra, but the flood could not have destroyed their treasury and thus the question of sending financial aid did not arise. However, as already discussed, from the treasury only copper coins were to be provided to those in severe distress (*su-atiyāyika*). It is difficult to explain whether this was refundable or non-refundable aid as we have not come across the treasury record. Our record is an official notification to the granary in-charge or in other words it is a granary record.

The Sohgaura bronze plaque is also an official granary record. However, we have not discovered any treasury records till date in the Indian subcontinent but the probability of finding one is enhanced by the reinterpretation of the Mahasthan fragmentary stone record. Such treasury records have been reported in large numbers from Persepolis in the Achaemenid empire discovered in 1933–4 and 1936–8. The Persepolis tablets are of immense importance.[1] These were mainly issued

[1]For the tablets from Persepolis also see Pierre Briant's *Histoire de l'Empireperse: De Cyrus à Alexandre*. Briant mentions that 'In 1933–34 and 1936–38, two batches of tablets were discovered in Persepolis by American excavators: the first in the N.E. corner of the terrace and the second in the S.E. section. Due to the locations of the finds, they are traditionally referred to as the Fortification Tablets (PF) and

under Darius I or Darius the Great (522–486 BCE) and his son Xerxes I (518–465 BCE). These tablets have been divided into two categories—treasury tablets and fortification tablets—based on their provenance. The former was found from the treasury area and the latter from the fortification walls.

These tablets bear testimony to an economic revolution and document the governmental mode of working with various payments and it is a transition period during the reign of Darius I when the government was switching from payment in kind to payment in cash (Cameron 1948: 4). Such elaborate documents were prepared while making payments in cash or kind from the treasury and other storages. Elamites were experts in bookkeeping, hence their help was taken to prepare these documents in Persepolis. The Persepolis texts can be broadly divided into two categories: 'Letter type', requesting the treasurer to pay the sum stipulated and 'Memorandum type' wherein workmen have already been paid by an individual and these documents were issued for reimbursement.

Though the case of these tablets is not similar to our record yet one thing is similar that there were storages for grains, flour, wine, oil and so on, which were under government control and the release of such from the storage required an order from the authorities. Payments stipulated by tablets found in the fortification at Persepolis are mostly in terms of goods like grains, flour, wine, oil or the like. It has been assumed by Cameron (1948: 4)

---

the Treasury Tablets (PT) respectively. These were published in 1948 by G.G. Cameron, who continued to publish them in the following years (PT 1957; PT 1963). There are 129 of them, dated between the 30th year of Darius (492) and the 7th year of Artaxerxes I (458)—apart from an Acadian tablet written in December 502 (PT 85). The Fortification lot—dated to the 13th to 28th years of Darius (509–494)—is much more imposing' (Briant 1996: 434).

that these tablets were tied to and accompanied the containers of such materials or goods. The Mahasthan fragmentary stone inscription too is a plaque which was an edict or a government notification ordering the release of grains from a granary to the people of another locality vide this particular token or plaque. Hence, this was a highly important official document. Since it was an official granary or a public granary, the accounting was very important. As we have mentioned earlier, similar to our document there would have been another document issued by the authorities to the treasury for the release of a particular sanctioned financial aid which was to be distributed very judiciously to those in dire necessity. This also reminds us of the Persepolis Treasury tablets vide which payments were made. The presence of such documents are rare in the Indian context and though not same or even similar yet the Mahasthan record is an exception and is a close parallel to the Persepolis tablets.

The Aśokan records, as already mentioned, were influenced by the Achaemenid inscribed records which were issued in multiple scripts and languages. Thus the making of the Mauryan inscriptional tradition owes to a large extent to the Achaemenid inscription and it is likely that besides the regular epigraphical records the Mauryas also had some awareness of the circulation of Achaemenid clay tablets in the northwestern border lands. This could have resulted in the use of portable, small clay tablets for administrative communications in the Mauryan times. Of course, the Mahasthan record is so far the only known specimen of a Mauryan clay tablet.

GAṆḌAKAS

Our record makes it clear that aid was in both cash and kind. Bhandarkar and Sircar both consider *gaṇḍakas* as coins (Bhandarkar 1931; Sircar 1966: 111). *Gaṇḍakas* mentioned in our grant have been taken as copper coins and as mentioned above this was a regional expression used in Bengal. It was also used in a much later epigraphic record of sixth century CE, the Faridpur grant of Dharmāditya which refers to the sale of land by taking two *dināras*, three *rūpakas* and six *gaṇḍakas*. The sequence in which they have been mentioned allows us to assume that since *dināras* mentioned here were gold coins probably of the Guptas, *rūpakas* were silver as the name suggests and the next which follows is assumed to be copper coins. As the record mentions *gaṇḍakas* and not *kārṣāpaṇas*, i.e. imperial silver punch-marked coins or to be precise Mauryan official currency, it seems that the money was the local currency circulating in the Vaṅga territory. The coins circulating here were local silver punch-marked coins of Wari-Bateshwar region. These were of high quality silver bearing four punches on the obverse and reverse of these coins were blank. Along with this early uninscribed cast copper coins were also in circulation. Probably these were referred to as *gaṇḍakas* in the record. We have shown in context that *gaṇḍaka* is a counting in four's and at the same time it denoted a coin/currency.

Mahasthan Coin Hoards and their Connection with the Record

From Mahasthan two hoards of imperial silver punch-marked coins have been reported which have been published in the First Interim Report of the excavation under the Bangladesh and French joint venture. The chapter on the coin hoard has been contributed by Marie-Françoise Boussac and Md. Shafiqul Alam (Boussac and Alam 2001: 229–64). She has identified the coins correctly according to the Gupta-Hardaker Catalogue (Gupta and Hardaker 1985). Another hoard from Mahasthan has been published by Bulbul Ahmed and Md. Noorul Islam and it has been named as Mahasthan Hoard II (Ahmed and Islam 2011). The nature of these two hoards from Mahasthan are very different. We shall discuss this below.

However, it is imperative to discuss here the relevance of these two hoards in studying the Mahasthan fragmentary record which is the prime focus of this monograph. The coins mentioned in the record are *gaṇḍakas* which are not silver punch-marked coins. We have already mentioned that *gaṇḍakas* might be copper coins and in our case these will be early uninscribed cast copper coins which have been reported from all over Bengal. They may also allude to copper punch-marked coins but these have not been reported in substantial quantity from excavations and explored contexts. Yet, we are discussing imperial silver punch-marked coins here, as it will help us to understand the region, its monetary history and also the relationship of northern part of Bengal with the Magadhan metropolitan area, to be precise how the Magadhan empire perceived and treated Bengal as a regional unit. This has always remained a lesser discussed topic probably due to a dearth of sources and mainly due to the fact that Bengal *per se* has hardly been considered as a significant region for understanding the character of the Mauryan empire. It becomes imperative to discuss the monetary history of early Bengal to understand its role and position from the imperial Magadhan perspective.

Coming back to the first two hoards published by Boussac and Alam, one from Mahasthan and the other from Baigacha. They draw our attention to the fact that the coins are of abnormally low weight.

1. *Mahasthan hoard*: Coins of this hoards are in silver and weigh mostly 2.1, 2.2, 2.3, 2.5 gm and two coins weigh 3 gm. Usually the imperial punch-marked coins are struck in the *kārṣāpaṇa* standard, weighing approximately 3.4 gm. However, the concentration point or the average weight of the coins of this hoard is 2.5 gm which is much lesser than the *kārṣāpaṇa* standard.
2. The Baigacha hoard also reflects a similar weight pattern. The coins in this hoard weigh between 1.7 and 2.9 gm. The concentration point or the average weight of this hoard is 2.41 gm, which is very close to 2.5 gm, which is the average weight of the Mahasthan hoard.

Boussac and Alam raised the question why these were issued in an abnormally low weight but they could find no satisfactory explanation. The present author has explained it elsewhere (Basu Majumdar 2018: 233–68) that this is a typical feature of Bengal and it probably indicates minting of these imperial punch-marked coins locally in Bengal. As the symbol combinations are just the same as that on an official Mauryan currency, the question arises as to why and how did the Mauryan administration allow and deal with this forgery or lesser weight coins once they were in circulation? The explanation is that it will allow such lesser weight coins to circulate along with the *kārṣāpaṇa* coins, only when the coining charges are sent to the imperial treasury by the locality or the subregion. In that case, the local authority after sending the coining charges or local minting charges deducted that amount from their coinage, to deal with the situation. It was dealt in two different ways: some of the subregions issued coins in lesser weight by subtracting the amount already remitted to the royal treasury at Magadha and the others decided to maintain the weight by increasing the alloy in the coinage. Hence, by debasing, they adjusted the deficit, i.e. already sent amount to the Magadhan territory (for such coins minted elsewhere see Fig. 4.4). The subregion of Varendra, which included the Mahasthan and Baigacha localities, opted for deducting the amount of precious metal and issuing coins in lesser weight but keeping the symbols intact.

Now, the third hoard, i.e. Mahasthan hoard (II) published by Ahmed and Hasan seems problematic. First, because it is mentioned as acquired from a coin dealer and the hoard was not from an excavated context, and second the coins are of normal weight. Both normal weight coins and lesser weight coins bearing same or similar symbols cannot circulate simultaneously. According to Gresham's law, bad money drives out good money hence, as soon as the lesser weight coins will be introduced in the market for circulation there will be a tendency to hoard the higher weight coins which can then be sold at the rate of precious metal and would fetch handsome money. More precisely, if coins containing a metal of different value have the same value as legal tender, the coins made of the cheaper metal will be used for payment, while those made of the more expensive metal will be hoarded or exported. It is against the law of monetization that two different weight coins of the same denomination would circulate at their intrinsic value in the same market. Hence, this proves beyond doubt that the Mahasthan hoard (II) which is mentioned by the authors to have acquired from a dealer originally belonged to some other locality or region and could not be from Varendra.

Coming back to the question of issuing coins locally, the Mauryans allowed the localities in Bengal to issue their own currency and circulate them locally. Probably when they paid taxes in these coins they would have accepted these metal pieces but prior to that the money-changers would have exchanged the money with imperial Mauryan punch-marked coins minted in the core or the metropolitan zone of the Magadhan empire. Even if they accepted it, they were rest assured that the coining fee was already remitted to the central royal treasury. Hence, despite the fact that these issues from Varendra were not of the same intrinsic value being less in weight, were accepted at their face value, i.e. equal to any other imperial punch-marked coin of *kārṣāpaṇa* standard.

This reminds one of the unique Persepolis treasury tablets from Iran published by Cameron where there was a discrepancy noticed in the coinage with which the payment of taxes was made to the royal treasury. In this case it was the initial phase of the transition from kind to cash in collection of taxes and it has been mentioned as 'economic revolution' by Cameron (1948: 4). However, the inscribed tablet under discussion is very interesting, it was inscribed in Akkadian Cuneiform script and it did not originate in Persepolis (Iran) (Cameron 1948: 4, 54). It is a record of re-evaluation of silver money submitted as tax by four individuals in the reign of Darius (19th–20th year) datable to 30 December 502 BCE. It this was the end of the financial year when the discrepancy was noticed. This was a precursor to the summoning of these four individuals to submit the deficit amount which was found to be 24 *shekels* in this case.[2] The above tablet reflects that at the end of the financial year or even while entering the money into the central treasury, coins were checked and weighed.

In case of the Mahasthan coins as well they would never pass the treasury test if the deficit amount was not

[2]The person submitted 8 *minas* and the money was found impure. It was 7½ *minas* 6 *shekels* and the loss of 24 *shekels* was discovered.

remitted to the royal treasury beforehand. Or one may have to assume that while sending them out of Bengal they were being converted into imperial currency of *kārṣāpaṇa* standard by the local authority prior to using them for paying consolidated taxes for the region.

The above discussion brings us to a more important question, i.e. why was Bengal issuing coins locally? The Mauryan central exchequer was unable to send adequate coinage for this region but the demand persisted. Hence, under the control of the local *mahāmātra* stationed at various localities of Bengal, the coining of pseudo-imperial coinage was taking place. It was the responsibility of the *mahāmātras* to convert and send the required amount to the central treasury as consolidated taxation from the region. What emerges very distinctly from the monetary patterns in Bengal is that each subregion adopted its own currency and the locality which was involved in more frequent interactions with the Magadhan metropolitan issued the closest replica of the coins, or in other words, imitated the coins of Magadha. This tendency of imitation continued in Bengal for a long time, at least up to the beginning of the early medieval century, one can notice the circulation of imitation or prototype coinage in Bengal (Basu Majumdar 2018).

When one looks at the Wari-Bateshwar complex or in the region of Vaṅga, one finds that they had their own local or *janapada* type punch-marked coinage. Their coinage was also influenced by the Magadha-Maurya punch-marked coins as they bear the sun and six-armed symbols which were found on the Mauryan coinage. Thus, the inspiration is quite distinct yet these coins bear four symbols which make them *janapada* type coins or local punch-marked coinage. Besides the sun and six-armed symbols there are two more symbols which vary. One finds

FIG. 4.3: Coins from Wari-Bateshwar

FIG. 4.4: Coins with increased alloy proportion issued from '*anyatra*' or outside the Mauryan territory

the representation of local culture of water and a fish-eating society on the coinage. We also find the depiction of symbols like fish, fish in hook, elephant-hunting (with a spear inserted on the body of the elephant), lobsters, boats and so on. Besides this, in the Vaṅga region we also find cast copper coins in excavated and explored contexts (see Fig. 4.3).

The fort of Mahasthan was built sometime in the Magadha-Maurya phase and our inscription also reflects the probable presence of a *mahāmātra* as the head or in-charge of the region. We do not have any evidence to support that there was a *kumāra* stationed at Puṇḍranagara or any other headquarter of a subregion in Bengal. Bengal was thus a part of Mauryan territory created with Mauryan support but the tendency was to extract revenue from this region. The intercommunication of these subregions as reflected from the Mahasthan fragmentary stone inscription is very interesting, and more striking is the interdependence. The locality of Puṇḍra was helping the subregion of Vaṅga and its neighbouring territories to combat the aftermath of flood. Whether this interdependence was locally decided or the instruction came from the central administration is a matter worth exploring.

5

In and Out of Emergency

BOTH THE Mahasthan and the Sohgaura records mention the term *atiyāyika* for indicating an emergency situation or calamity. *Atiyāyika* is an emergency situation requiring immediate help not suffering any delay. The Mahasthan fragmentary stone inscription is an order issued from Puṇḍranagara to the local office in the *Saṁvargīya* locality which was affected by flood. As two types of emergencies have been mentioned in the record, we have assumed that the person who would like to avail the aid would have to mention the reason whether it was for *dagatiyāyika* or *suatiyāyika* while taking financial aid from the treasury or paddy from the storehouse. While the grant of paddy was a general grant, financial aid was specifically for those intensely affected by calamity. Since two separate government offices were involved, the instruction might have reached or communicated in clear terms to these two offices and the officers concerned.

Arthaśāstra (4.3.1) mentions eight types of disasters, viz., that caused by fire (*agni*), flood (*udaka*), disease or epidemic (*vyādhi/maraka*), drought (*durbhikṣa*), disaster caused by rats (*mūṣika*) or by beasts (*vyāla)* or by snake bites (*sarpa*) and calamities caused by demons/tribes (*rākṣasa*) (Kangle II 2014: 262). The natural calamities caused due to divine interventions were beyond the control of humans—*daivapīḍanaṁ-agnir udakaṁ vyādhir durbhikṣaṁ maraka iti* (*Arthaśāstra* 8.4.1). With time the concept of disasters and their management became more and more complex as in the fourth century CE, we find a much more elaborate list of disasters in the *Kāmandakīya Nītisāra* (Dutt 1896). This text categorizes disasters into fifteen divisions as compared to eight in the *Arthaśāstra*. These are disasters caused due to excessive rain, drought, locusts, rats, mice, parrots (and other crop destroying agents), unjust taxation, unlawful punishment, foreign invasion, thieves and robbers, failure to control royal ministers, epidemics, diseases among humans and diseases among cattle. As already discussed in the list of natural disasters, i.e. *daivapīḍana*, Kauṭilya discusses those caused due to fire (*agni*), flood (*udaka*), epidemic (*vyādhi*) and *maraka* and drought (*durbhikṣa*),[1] these have been mentioned as natural and uncontrollable disasters. The expression '*upanipāta-pratīkāra*' (*Arthaśāstra* 4.3) in the *Arthaśāstra* is synonymous with prevention or remedy for a sudden and unexpected attack or breaking forth of an unexpected calamity.

There are a few primary calamities which may lead to urban disasters and sufferings like epidemics and famine caused as an aftermath of natural disasters like flood and drought respectively. Such secondary disasters have long-

[1] '*daivapīḍanaṁ-agnir udakaṁ vyādhir durbhikṣaṁ maraka iti*', *Arthaśāstra* 8.4.1.

term effect on society and on human lives. Often such famines are named after the place name where the outbreak had taken place, for example the text *Meṇḍakāvadāna* provides us with reference to famines categorized into three groups, viz., *Cañcu*, *Śvetāsthi* and *Śalākavṛtti*, of these the first one was a place name and it is also mentioned in the Sohgaura bronze plaque inscription. It has been mentioned in the *Meṇḍakāvadāna* that during the *Cañcu*, people were compelled to survive on grains, which were collected in a box for appeasing the dead. During the *Śvetāsthi* famine, people used to boil the bones which they collected from different places until the bones became totally white and drank this soup. During the *Śalākavṛtti* famine which was worst among the three, grains and molasses stuck up in holes/drainage holes were taken out with the help of sticks and boiled with large quantities of water and the soup thus prepared formed the food for famine-stricken populace. We have seen in the Sohgaura bronze plaque inscription that *Cañcu* is mentioned as a place from where the grains and other commodities were to be brought and stored at the two storehouses. This may indicate that the famine had not struck *Cañcu* by then and may be the forecast of a famine had led the government to prepare for the forthcoming famine.

These two records when taken together in the context of calamity or disaster and their management in the early historic period, especially under the Mauryas, provide us with significant insight. For such organized administrative structure and disaster management, a state-controlled economic system and an all-pervasive administrative machinery is required and the presence of both is attested in these two records. The state adopted a positive attitude to mitigate the troubles of famine-affected regions. We thus come across a public policy to combat disaster and other elements of famine relief policy which were also developed by the state. The regional and local centres were involved in the process of disbursement of grains and cash.

Aśokan records also mention the term *atiyāyika*. A major Rock Edict VI mentions the following:

yaṁ pi cā kichi mukhate ānapayāmi hakaṁ dāpakaṁ vā sāvakaṁ vā ye vā punā mahāmatehi atiyāyike ālopite hoti tāyeṭhāye vivāde nijhati vā saṁtaṁ palisāye anaṁtaliyenā paṭi...viye me savatā sabaṁ kālaṁ (Ll. 18–19).

And also, if in the council (of *Mahāmātras*) a dispute arises, or an amendment is moved, in connetion (connection) with any donation or proclamation which I am ordering verbally, or (in connexion [connection] with) an emergent matter which has been delegated to the *Mahāmātras*, it must be reported to me immediately, anywhere, (and) at any time (Hultzsch 1991: 34–5).

It is interesting to note that the term *atiyāyika* is found in the *Arthaśāstra* and the Aśokan edicts, whereas in the *Dharmasāstras* one comes across the use of the term *āpad/ āpaddharma*. The term *āpad* also denotes calamity/hard times/difficulty/danger/misfortune/distress or adversity and *āpaddharma* is the practice only allowable in time of distress.

In the context of emergency it may be pointed out that the *Arthaśāstra* also mentions emergency financing or taxation to replenish the depleted treasury. Such taxations which were imposed during an emergency is mentioned as *praṇaya*. *Praṇaya* is a demand for grains, money, etc. which were extracted as additional levies imposed by the state, in case the treasury got depleted. This was done with a purpose to raise resources by imposing exorbitant tax regimes. Such taxes were probably imposed on the regions which were not affected by the calamity as such, but it was imposed on the rest of the regions or subregions within the empire to overcome the calamity. However, our inscription does not bear any reference to such a *praṇayakriyā*.

SUATIYĀYIKA

Our record also mentions the term *suatiyāyika* which we have taken as intense emergency.[2] The prefix '*su*' is usually taken to denote 'good'. But here in our case it refers to intensive, 'very', 'extremely'. Especially with words that refer to something bad or hurtful, the prefix *su*—is added to increase the intensity of the expression like *sukrodha*—very angry; *sutapas*—extreme asceticism or practicing severe austerity, etc. So according to Olivelle *su-ātyāyika* can, and probably does, mean: an extreme emergency.

Another interesting factor is that the city of Puṇḍranagara (modern Mahasthan), was the seat of the *mahāmātra*. This *nagara* lent its name to a larger territory which was designated as Pauṇḍravardhana (Puṇḍravardhana) which is mentioned as a *bhukti* in several epigraphic records. The case of Puṇḍranagara giving the name to a larger territory of Puṇḍravardhana reminds us of a similar case in early historic Chhattisgarh wherein the village of Kosalā lent its name to the larger territory of Kosalā, which was the seat of the Śarabhapurīyas, Pāṇḍuvaṁśins and Somavaṁśins (Basu Majumdar 2017: 119–29).

[2]The present author is thankful to Prof. Patrick Olivelle who has suggested this meaning for the term *suatiyāyika*.

6

The Mahasthan Record Reassessed

THE FOREGOING discussions prove beyond doubt that this was a government order or an administrative order issued by an authority, probably the storekeeper of the granary, located at Puṇḍranagara, i.e. Mahasthan, to disburse grains for the *Saṁvargīyas*, who were facing a natural calamity. The inscription is very well constructed not only from the linguistic point of view but also its content and execution. This being the first record from undivided Bengal surprises us, as there is no parallel before or after this record.

The next set of records from Bengal are the early historic seals and sealings. Several such seals and sealings have been discovered from the sites like Chandraketugarh, Deganga, Mahasthan, Tomluk, Harinarayanpur, Pandurajar Dhibi, Tilpi and so on which may be assigned to the early historic phase. Other than this record, we only have another record from Shilua, in Noakhali district of Bangladesh, which is a stone image inscription in Brāhmī. But the inscription is highly corroded and cannot be deciphered (Islam, II, 2018: 608). There may be some records from Silimpur that might fall into this category, but they still remain unpublished.[1] Hence, it is difficult to include them in the list of early historic records from Bengal, at the present state of our knowledge. A comprehensive corpus of early historic records from Bengal is a desideratum. The above discussion strengthens the probability of the Mahasthan record being issued by an administrative officer stationed at Puṇḍranagara if not directly from Magadhan metropolitan zone.

The order for giving grains, i.e. paddy, would have come from the metropolitan, i.e. Pāṭaliputra, to the *mahāmātra* stationed at Puṇḍranagara, who after receiving such an instruction might have ordered the creation of such a government order. A similar order, in all probability, was also created for the officer in-charge of the treasury (*koṣa*) to release financial aid as and when necessary. The order for financial aid would have been more precise as there was involvement of money, and its accounting was extremely important. The aid was to be provided locally, hence, the treasury in all probability was located in the territory of the *Saṁvaṅgīyas* and not in Puṇḍranagara. It is indeed interesting that the financial aid is mentioned not as *kārṣāpaṇa* in the record but as *gaṇḍaka*. *Gaṇḍaka* is a region specific term for indicating copper coins and its use was limited to Bengal, which again reflects that the money for the financial aid was not huge and was not released from the metropolitan Magadha.

What is more intriguing is that one subregion of Bengal was extending aid to another, and if this happened at the

[1]The present author is thankful to Dr Rajat Sanyal for this information.

orders of the Magadhan imperial authority it is one of the earliest evidences of inter-subregional communication and exchange indicating some kind of dependency. At this juncture, it is imperative to examine the other sources to understand the position of these subregions in the early historic phase. Mahasthan and Bangarh were two important or prominent urban centres in the subregion of Varendra in the early historic phase and in the same way if we consider the *Saṁvaṅgīya* to be a group of people of the Vaṅga subregion, then Wari-Bateshwar was a major urban centre in this zone. Compared to Mahasthan, the settlement at Wari-Bateshwar was much smaller as has been already discussed, but both came into existence in *c.*fourth century BCE as urban settlements.

As we have already discussed above, the term *Saṁvaṁgīya* denoted the people of the subregion of Vaṅga or their confederacy. Hence the flood affected zone was in this subregion. It is not necessary that the whole subregion was affected by flood. While mentioning the urban centres in this subregion we have mentioned the complex or the twin villages which formed the urban centre, i.e. the present day Wari and Bateshwar. In this context, it is interesting to note that in a recently published research article by Muhammad Kamal Hossenakanda et al. based on grain size and clay mineralogical analyses it is suggested that Wari-Bateshwar was a settlement or localities of settlements in a flood-prone zone (Hossenakanda et al. 2015: 15–39). According to the authors, the fluvio-locational advantages for mercantile activities during the 'early historic' period ceased to exist after the significant changes. There is reference to floods in this zone in the early historic phase, affecting the settlement and there seems to be a large gap. The possible factors of this temporal gap mentioned by them are factors induced by alluvial environment caused by flood, changes in the river course, impact of neotectonism, southward shifting of the estuarine belt shoreline and so on. To be precise, they suggest a temporal gap between the 'early historic' and 'early medieval' period in the area. The authors mention that 'the inhabitants of these settlements had to negotiate with the changing alluvial landscape, channel dynamics, fluvial regime, relative sea level, migration of shoreline and above all, floods' (Hossenakanda et al. 2015: 36). They propose the hypothesis that Wari-Bateshwar was occupied and abandoned and the fortified settlement was predominantly developed for mercantile purposes (Hossenakanda et al. 2015: 36). This strengthens our hypothesis and enhances the probability of Wari-Bateshwar being the urban centre of the Vaṅga subregion mentioned in our record where aid was sent from Puṇḍranagara.

At Mahasthan the excavations conducted over several years have brought a very significant fact to light that the urban settlement here was created due to its contact with the Ganga valley and the settlers of period I in this region are termed as 'pioneers' by Alam and Salles, who state that they brought with them a pottery culture which was alien to the region of Bengal—the northern black polish ware luxury pottery (Alam and Salles 2001). There are several other elements which travelled to this region of Pundranagara with the Magadhan contact and this urban settlement was created due to Mauryan impetus. The urban settlement here can very well be designated as a case of secondary urbanization (Chattopadhyaya 2003: 66–101). The presence of an urban centre with the use of money and diverse artisanal activities is noticeable at Mahasthan. Besides this, it had a large fortification. Such fortification involved the use of thousands of bricks which reflects labour-intensive activities and also the presence of a large population here. Though the city of Puṇḍranagara (Mahasthan) was almost half the size of the Mauryan capital at Pāṭaliputra, which Habib and Jha mention as Grade III following F.R. Allchin's methodology of assessing inhabited areas of the Mauryan period (Habib and Jha 2005: 126). As per this assessment, the approximate population density of Mahasthan in the third century BCE, would have been around 72,000, whereas the same at Pāṭaliputra would have been 140,000. The settlement archaeology of Mahasthan reflects wealthy houses. The presence of the fortified city definitely could not have survived without a supplying hinterland and other economic institutions, markets, currency, traders and so on. This indirectly also points out to the presence of a structured administrative set-up, a proper defensive mechanism, surplus or adequate resources to divert sufficient resource for labour and materials to create, maintain and sustain public structures. We can notice a well-organized state apparatus with hierarchy. The above analysis of the Mahasthan record has revealed that the order probably for the release of grains from the granary at Mahasthan came from metropolitan Magadha and the officer stationed here was also a Magadhan recruit (if the term is taken to be *mahāmātra*). *Mahāmātra* is specifically an administrative officer of the Mauryans and with a single exception from Bengal, the mention of *mahāmātras* is not found in any other dynasty or any other time frame. We find the officer named *mahāmātra* mentioned among the functionaries in the Aśokan edicts and this officer also finds mention in Kauṭilīya's *Arthaśāstra*, portions of which were composed in the third century BCE. In our case, the official instruction to release crops and cash from the storehouse and treasury for an afflicted community, may imply the storage facilities of certain commodities in official storehouses located in the urban centres.

If this granary is considered to be an official storage of general category and not a specific one, as in the case of Sohgaura, which was only for emergency purposes, then it reflects resource mobilization through an efficient revenue machinery. It is likely that these commodities reached the storehouse through revenue measures, which were taken in kind as tax (*bhāga*), given as stipulated share of the produce demanded by the Mauryan administration. Such taxes were collected by the *mahāmātras* employed by the Mauryan state. Mahasthan inscription hence, gives a clearcut picture of penetration of the state society in the subregions of Varendra and Vaṅga in the third century BCE.

One of the salient markers of a state society is the use of writing and the employment of scripts to facilitate record-keeping and communications which are essential elements in the making of a large territorial polity. The Mahasthan record is one of the most important evidences to such record-keeping in writing, with a certain amount of durability (as the medium used was stone). As far as Bengal is concerned, there was no urban settlement prior to *c.*fourth century BCE. One may argue that there existed no *mahājanapadas* in this eastern extremity, as the list of *mahājanapadas* in the *Aṅguttaranikāya* does not mention any territorial unit from Bengal. However, the presence of *janapadas* in Bengal is attested by the rich numismatic evidence that comes from the early historic phase. The early coins from Bengal which may be dated to *c.*third century BCE, clearly reflect the existence of small territorial units or *janapadas* with a certain amount of autonomy, as they minted their own currencies both in silver and in copper.

This small record at Mahasthan also reflects that there existed a hierarchized and complex polity. The subregion of Varendra had a well-defined territory and population with a proper administrative set-up, officers of varied levels, monetary system, tax assessment, record-keeping and resource mobilization. All these were also partially present in Vaṅga subregion. These features of state-based polity, of course, were imbibed by these subregions from the Magadhan state. This clearly reflects the Mauryan political control over these subregions of Bengal. The level of control varied due to several factors. Puṇḍranagara's proximity to Pāṭaliputra made it more vibrant and connected with the metropolitan Magadha and this is clearly reflected in the monetary system of this subregion. The control over Vaṅga was less intense, as it was comparatively far and difficult to manage due to its typical geographical conditions. It was issuing its own currency and was not directly dependent on the supply of coins from Magadha.

As far as the two subregions are concerned, with which the Mahasthan record is connected, i.e. Varendra and Vaṅga, it is also imperative to discuss how other literary sources mention them. As already discussed above, Vaṅga denotes a group of people. Even in the *Aitareya Āraṇyaka* they are mentioned as a group of people associated with the Magadhans (Keith 1967: 200). They are mentioned in the *Baudhāyana Dharmasūtra* as one of the people living outside Āryāvarta (Bhattacharyya 1977: 56; Olivelle 2000: 198). Vaṅga people are also referred to in the *Rāmāyaṇa*, *Arthaśāstra*, *Mahābhāṣya* of Patañjali, *Digvijaya* section of *Mahābhārata*, *Mahāniddesa*, *Milindapañha* and so on (Chowdhury and Alam 2018: 23). *Arthaśāstra* (2.11.102-104) mentions cotton from Vaṅga (Kangle, I, 2014: 55). *Mahāniddesa* and *Milindapañha* indicate that there was a coastal area approachable from the sea in the territory of Vaṅga. It is difficult to ascertain the exact territory of Vaṅga in different periods. It broadly denoted areas in the south and southeastern part of Bangladesh. Vaṅga usually denotes the areas between the two main streams of Ganga, from Bhagirathi to the Padma-Meghna. According to B.N. Mukherjee, the earliest connotation of Vaṅga consisted of a larger territory which included the modern districts of 24-Parganas, Hooghly, Howrah, Medinipur and parts of Bardhaman along with the coastal region of present-day Bangladesh up to the mouth of Padma (Mukherjee 2000: 12). Puṇḍras, who were an autochthonous community of north Bengal, are found mentioned in the Vedic corpus but with some disdain.

The Mahasthan and Sohgaura plaque inscriptions when taken together, not only provide us with an insight into the relief measures carried out by the state apparatus, but also help us to understand the attitude of the state in dealing with calamities. The efficiency and concern of the Mauryan state in carrying out such relief measures, not only as a part of philanthropic activities, but with a farsighted vision to run the state in a more systematic manner and ensure that such calamities do not have any major impact on the revenue collection of the state, comes out distinctly. The two sites of Mahasthan and Sohgaura were different from each other. Mahasthan was an urban centre where the collection and distribution of agricultural resources was done. Its pivotal position in famine relief operations indicate that it was a nodal point or settlement locality which again consisted of a network of local settlements (Chattopadhyaya 2003). Sohgaura was located on a nodal point or junction. Though it revealed features of an urban centre, yet, one has to look at the size, settlement structure and linkages across space.

An assessment of all these factors reflect that it was not an urban centre but just a junction on the highway, mainly for the purpose of collection of toll.

In the Vaṅga region, the soil type is calcareous alluvium, peat and non-calcareous dark grey flood plain soil and in such soil paddy of aman, boro, kaon and, among other, crops like maize, barley, banana, mustard, jute, etc. usually grow. The dry land rabi crops can only be grown if floodwater recedes before December. Our record refers to a post-flood situation and as one may assume that the flood which struck the Saṁvaṅgīyas as a calamity would have been in the months of June or July, i.e. the monsoon season. The local people might have been heavily affected and would have lost their paddy reserves for sowing their rabi crop. The relief measure mentioned in our record was probably to combat this situation and sow seeds for a rabi crop. Such a crop would grow some time in December for which the aid was probably provided.

7

Querying the Empire

> The formation and structure of empires can be examined more meaningfully if the empire is seen as a further and more evolved form of the state.
>
> THAPAR (1981: 410)

AN EMPIRE has a large territorial expanse and it also accommodates many diversities and unevenness. The complex process of accommodating and balancing the divergences without ironing out the complexities and unevenness or imbalances, needs a far more complex socio-political organization and machinery. This becomes a key factor in bringing it to the level of an empire. The term 'empire' has been used often in an indiscriminate manner. Empires in early India were mainly named after dynasties and our query concerns the Mauryan empire. Though no Mauryan record has been reported from Bengal so far, yet scholars are unanimous about the inclusion of Bengal within the Mauryan empire. The stone tablet which forms the central theme of this monograph is surprisingly the only early historic inscription from undivided Bengal other than the seals and sealings. It does not mention any Mauryan ruler and the only word on the basis of which this record is more or less declared Mauryan is a broken word which reads '*māte*', reconstructed as *mahāmāte*, i.e. a Mauryan official *mahāmātra*.[1] However, besides this, on the basis of several other factors we have discussed the Mauryan-ness of our record in the previous chapters.

Sovereignty is the key to an empire and absolute sovereignty meant right to collect taxes, wage wars and secure uniformity in the legal procedures throughout the empire or to make specific laws for specific communities and situations. The making of the Mauryan empire involved the acquisition of an extensive territory either appropriated or acquired through conquests. Besides this extensive territory, the other features of this empire are centralized administration, the king as the apex political authority, officers appointed to maintain law, regular revenue assessment and tax collection mechanism controlled by the state, attempts to secure cultural uniformity through a common script, language, rituals and festivals and above all a common currency. Centralized administration which is mentioned above as a key feature, however, does not indicate a monolithic administration, it rather indicates a control over revenue collection and

[1]The Mahasthan stone tablet is also not very different from the rest of the early historic records as one may consider it as a tablet or a large seal which was an administrative notification. It is very neatly engraved and well formulated, considering its early date and the fact that it is till date the earliest record from Bengal. Besides this, the record and its analysis clearly reflect that Bengal or at least a major portion of undivided Bengal including Varendra and Vaṅga formed a part of the Mauryan territory.

appropriation of resources. The dynamics of power between the metropolitan zone and the regions from where the revenues would flow into the central treasury became the deciding factor on which the rigidness and flexibility of relationships rested upon. The officials posted at the provincial levels ensured the transfer of the collected revenue mainly from agrarian sources in their provinces to the centre. The uniformity in administration was sought to a certain extent and economic appropriation was the basic motive.

The Mauryan empire evolved from pre-existing states and communities which more or less maintained an independent status prior to their inclusion into the former. The Magadhan territory from which the Mauryas rose to power, was always considered as their power base. This is reflected in the use of a very simple title by Aśoka with an allusion to the principal territory or their power base, i.e. '*rājā Māgadhe*' (as found in the Bhabru edict of Aśoka. Also see Thapar 2005: 161, 2013: 231). However, the Mauryans did not take elaborate imperial titles, it was always *devānaṁpriya*, i.e. beloved of the gods. Even after having a control over a huge territory from Afghanistan in the northwest to Karnataka in the south and Girnar-Sopara in the west to Dhauli-Jaugada in the east which was at times designated as Jambudvīpa yet Aśoka himself uses the simplistic title of *rājā Māgadhe* which clearly shows that the control over this base was stronger or dominant than the rest of the regions and subregions within the political control of the Mauryan empire. Thapar draws our attention to the sharp contrast with the minor ruling powers who soon after coronation took elaborate titles like *mahārājādhirāja* and so on. This has led her to conclude that 'clues to the empire need not lie in royal titles' (Thapar 2013: 231). The relationship between the Mauryan empire and its constituent provincial units depended on the nature of the provinces and their economic resource base, mainly agrarian and mineral resources. Thapar mentions the relationship with the periphery also as 'internal colonialism' (Thapar 2013: 225). The regions, however, were not colonies but were provinces with nuclei often in twins, like Tosali and Samāpā in Kaliṅga.

The emergence or the making of a complex institution like a state, involves the transformation of a relatively simpler society to a sharply differentiated and hierarchized one. This involves the introduction of change at several levels like the political, socio-economic and cultural milieu in different periods and various regions (Thapar 2005; Allchin 1995). In case of Bengal (undivided), issuance of a local currency clearly reflects the continued manifestation of the 'autonomous spaces' within the ambit of the state through regions. It is not possible to look for a centralized, all-powerful, pervasive state in this case (Chattopadhyaya 2022: 68–80).

Bengal interacted in varied ways with the complex societies which led to its passage into the domain of a state society. The Magadhan connection was the prime factor and the Mauryan empire driven by its interests in resources, like elephants, timber, medicinal herbs, and an easy access to the coast, led to the extension of its control over this region of Bengal. Moreover, to maintain a strong grip over Kaliṅga it was imperative to have a strong control over the neighbouring territory of Bengal and maintain peace and congenial relations with that territory. The region of Bengal formed the easternmost boundary of the Mauryan empire. The acquisition of this region of economic potential both in terms of agricultural and commercial from which revenue would flow into the metropolitan area was hence quite important for the

Mauryan state. Thapar divides the Mauryan state into three segments: the metropolitan state, core areas and peripheries. The control of the state was differentially present or varied across regions and localities (Thapar 1987: 1–30). The location of major rock edicts of Aśoka are on the boundaries of the Mauryan territory almost defining the geographical extent of the empire. The question which arises here is that if Bengal was the easternmost boundary of the Mauryan empire then why is there an absence of major rock edicts in Bengal? One may argue that the easternmost boundary was represented by the two Kaliṅga edicts but that does not solve the issue as the Kaliṅgan region had an altogether separate entity and was not associated with the territory of Bengal. Hence ideally there should have been two major rock edict sites in Bengal as all these were issued in twins. Bengal lacks such free-standing stones and mountain ranges which may be one of the reasons for the absence of major rock edicts or they might have been destroyed if they were sent in free-standing stones like the Sannati edicts (Basu Majumdar 2016).

However, Bengal was not a periphery like the southern territory (consisting of sites in present-day Karnataka and Andhra Pradesh) from where gold reserves, minerals and other surplus were sent to the metropolis and the region did not witness any considerable material restructuring or significant development. The policy of extraction dominated here. In case of Bengal, at least at Mahasthan, one notices that the urban centre developed due to the Magadhan linkage. It is difficult to ascertain how much autonomy was provided to the local chieftains in the southern territory of the Mauryas, but in case of Bengal it was quite different. In Bengal, the presence of autonomous spaces within the region is very prominent and their inclusion into the state society was smoothly executed by the appointment of Mauryan officials at the apex of local administration. The presence of *mahāmātra* at Puṇḍranagara and the carrying out of orders of the state in helping another autonomous space, i.e. Vaṅga, can only take place with the political cohesiveness with the metropolitan. Usually, such autonomy is seen in case of the foresters where not much political restructuring is done but a strict control is maintained which is reflected in the strong admonition in tone of the emperor while cautioning the *āṭavikas* (Chakravarti 2016: 160). But in case of Bengal there does not seem to be much of ideological confrontation like that in the case of the state and the forest where the zeal for civilizing the barbarians can be noticed.

The case of Bengal clearly reflects that the Mauryan state recognized its diversity. It did not encourage equality between the diverse communities and allowed them to maintain their own respective identities to a great extent. However, the Mahasthan record clearly reflects that this unity was achieved by enhancing intra-regional communication and interdependence of the subregional units. This interlinking of differentiated systems within a peripheral area would also have modified the impact of the metropolitan state. While discussing the Mauryan empire, Thapar also mentions that the metropolitan state, i.e. Magadha proper, was the most important element and the control over the rest of the provinces was flexible. The relationship between the metropolitan and the rest of the regions was at times so loose that one may even lose sight of a distinct overarching empire. While discussing this issue, Thapar almost goes to the extent to clarify her position that she was not arguing in favour of the notion that 'there was no empire'. It is courtesy the vision of

Aśoka who engraved the records to document his presence or to make the empire visible that one gets the feel of this colossal empire. If the epigraphic records are kept aside then one can hardly imagine that how huge and colossal was the extent of the Mauryan empire.

One of the major element of a state or/and an empire is maintaining an efficient administrative set-up where most of the employees are salaried. A similar economic pressure on the empire was that of maintaining an elaborate army. Facilitating the army with smooth travel and communication on a public expenditure was the duty of the empire. The region of Bengal with its peculiar hydrography was most difficult to control and maintaining an army here would be a major economic drain on the metropolitan state.

As we have seen, the subregions of Bengal were allowed to mint their own coinage, which were Mauryan in appearance, yet their metallic composition and weights varied. This was a type of autonomy which was provided to Bengal alone. It is very difficult to assess at this moment why was Bengal allowed this autonomy. Along with the Mauryan prototype coins, some of the subregions in Bengal also issued their own local currencies parallel to the Mauryan coinage, like the Chandraketugarh, Wari-Bateshwar and Tamralipta complex (Basu Majumdar 2018: 233–68). It is the richness of the soil of Bengal and its productive nature, the delta and the access to the sea, its easy communication linkages due to the riverine networks, the presence of natural resources, elephants in large numbers, all these factors might have made it quite lucrative to the Magadhans. At the same time the hydrography of Bengal and its delta made it problematic as it was a flood-prone zone. Its communication network was quite different in nature and hence it was difficult to handle from the metropolitan zone. The autonomy would have yielded better results for the Magadhan territory as this enabled them to procure revenue from this region without facing the hazards and without bearing the cost of maintaining an army. This again makes Bengal another kind of peripheral zone. In this case, one is reminded of the perception of the Greeks about this easternmost territory. Though the Greeks would never have visited this region but their perception of this coastal deltaic Bengal (Gangaridae) was that it had a separate identity from that of Magadha. They were aware that it was the easternmost region and beyond this existed the Bay of Bengal and also the fact that this region was rich in elephants (Chowdhury, I, 2018).

Political dismemberment can be distinctly noticed in case of the region of Bengal, which has been taken as the existence of autonomous spaces within the empire. This can be clearly seen through a thorough study of its monetary history. Though there would have been attempts at introducing universality of currency yet when compared to other regions and subregions, Bengal stands out. The monetary divisiveness reflects the existence of segmented cultural dismemberment or autonomous spaces within the region. The cohesiveness and the tension that existed in the relationship between the various subregions is quite interesting and intriguing. It was brought under the umbrella of the Mauryan empire by the introduction of a common currency issued in a fixed weight standard of *kārṣāpaṇa*, but in Bengal this Mauryan official currency coexisted with the local currency. The presence of both local and imperial currencies as medium of exchange probably indicates the existence of dual control. The local or supra-local (as in the case of Saṁvaṅgīya[2]) control over the subregional communities led them to issue and use a local medium of exchange, i.e. local coins. At subregional levels the people might have paid taxes in local currency. The use of imperial coins was mainly by and for the local authority (*mahāmātra*) to enable him to remit taxes to the centre in a universal mode of payment. In case of Bengal, issuance of a local currency clearly reflects the continued manifestation of the autonomous spaces within the ambit of the state through regions.

It is not possible to look for the control of a centralized, all-powerful, pervasive state in this case. Here we may cite Chattopadhyaya who questions the extent to which the community/communities were integrated into the state structure and to what extent they were at a 'distance' from this structure is not very distinct while discussing the problem of the demarcation of spaces of authority (Chattopadhyaya 2022: 68–80). The autonomous spaces within the structure of a state and their political and social structure can be understood by exploring the dynamics of the resources of autonomous authority and the interest of the authority of the state in procuring those resources. In no way the authority of the autonomous spaces were contradictory to the authority of the state (Bongard-Levin and Vigasin 1978–9: 16–30).

When one looks at the Mahasthan record as an administrative notification and an instrument of instruction, it comes out loud and clear that in such cases of emergency, the attitude of the Mauryan state was to extend help. Such aid involved financial resources hence their documentation at different levels was quite

[2]The locality of Vaṅga was a conglomeration of smaller localities which formed the Saṁvaṅgīya territory or a greater Vaṅga.

important for record-keeping and also for final accounting. A parallel is found in the Sohgaura bronze plaque record from Gorakhpur area, as already discussed, but what is to be reconsidered is the use of two different mediums for recording similar aids. In case of Sohgaura, it was documented on a bronze plaque, which is strange, as much later a similar metallic medium (i.e. copperplate charters) was adopted for issuing land grants. But more than 500 years before the issuance of land grants in copperplates, this record was issued in bronze plates. It was a notification to be nailed on the door of the granary, yet its size was too small (like that of a tablet) to be noticed.

We have already addressed the issue of why the Mahasthan record was incised on stone, yet it needs to be mentioned here that there was a need to issue a record with durability, as it involved a transaction from the treasury and granary, which were state-owned. Moreover, when the annual inspection would take place, it would be important to justify the absence of a certain amount of grains from the public granary and this record would be the document that the *mahāmātra* would produce in favour of this absence, as per this official order. Since this was not for display and not meant to be nailed on the door of the granary, but to be kept safely, it was issued on a durable material like stone.

The fresh reading and interpretation have brought to light the names of two officials who were involved in the execution of the relief activity or extending aid by a subregion to another, probably at the instruction of the state authorities, from the Magadhan central administration. Mauryan documents usually do not bear the names of officials.[3] Even the *āryaputra* who was

[3]Rest of the names like that of queen Kāruvāki and Tīvara ('*Tīvala mātu Kāluvāki*') were Aśoka's own decision and he mentions them (Queen's Edict in Allahabad Pillar).

stationed at Suvarṇagiri (Karnataka), as the regional head, is not mentioned by his name. In this case, the mention of these two officials by their personal names is an exception.[4] However, we have to remember that the Mahasthan record itself is not a general one and is enigmatic. Here, the names occur as a precautionary measure. As such type of aids were not regular these were exceptional cases involving financial handlings. If by chance there was a change in the official position of the local authority (i.e. *mahāmātra*), either due to termination of service or transfer, if any dispute arose or discrepancy was noticed while checking or tallying the annual records/ accounts, the person in-charge of the transaction could be summoned.

It was an important task of the state to maintain detailed accounts of each and every taxation that entered the granaries and the treasuries. The treasurer and the chief collector of revenue were the two most important offices in the Magadhan administrative set up, as is reflected even in the *Arthaśāstra*. These two offices were in all probability controlled by the central administration. The treasurers were responsible for keeping an account of the income in cash and also for storing the income in kind, as revenue was paid both in cash and kind. This reflects a dual system of calculation which involved the conversion of the kind in cash for record-keeping purpose. Such a situation arose when money is recently introduced and the age old practice of accepting revenue in kind has not been done away with. Hence, both continue simultaneously. Moreover a share of the produce which was to be paid as revenue also would have been accepted in kind. Such records were kept by the chief collector, who was assisted by a body of clerks. They kept account of the taxes that

[4]If we consider both Taladina and Dumadina as *mahāmātras*.

came to the royal treasury from various parts of the empire. Thus, the granary in-charge and the treasury in-charge had to work in close association maintaining a coordination with each other as taxes were also paid in kind and their accounting was done in cash.

Taxation was the prime concern of the state, as it had to maintain a large army and for this purpose tax was imposed on every possible taxable commodity. It was considered a state prerogative to enhance the production of crops by bringing more cultivable land into the domain of the Magadhan empire and also by looking at irrigation facilities. Irrigation was one of the prime areas where the Mauryan imperial authority invested a large sum of money. This also reflects that getting more returns from the produce was the prime concern of the state. Similarly, our record which is a management of a crisis situation and to ensure good crop in future, also seems to be an initiative of the state, to ensure good produce after the flood waters receded and the situation improved. It was an attempt not only to combat the situation and bring the lives of people of Bengal to normalcy, but also to ensure that the revenue which this agriculturally-rich zone of Bengal generated for the Magadhan empire remained unaffected.

An appraisal of the Mahasthan record in the light of other available sources, especially the numismatic specimens from Bengal, very clearly brings forth the picture of the Mauryan empire as a complex form of state which accommodated culturally different people and different political and economic systems (Thapar 2015: 141–71). The regions, though different from the Mauryan framework in variable degrees were situated within the Mauryan empire. The dynamics and equations between the state and the regions depended on factors like the location dynamics, resources, resource mobilization, cultural differences and power politics. Bengal emerged as a region with relatively more local-level autonomy with varied or multiple subregional relationship dynamics making it very close yet very distant from the Mauryan state.

Select Bibliography

Primary Sources

TEXTS (ORIGINAL AND TRANSLATION)

Kangle, R.P. (2014). *The Kauṭilīya Arthaśāstra*, Part II, Bombay: University of Bombay (1st edn. 1963).

Dutta, M.N. (1896). *Kāmandakīya Nītisāra*, Calcutta: Elysium Press.

Keith, A.B. (ed. and tr.) (1967). *Aitareya Āraṇyaka*, London: Oxford University Press.

Olivelle, P. (ed. and tr.) (2000). *Dharmasūtras: The Law Codes of Āpastamba, Gautama, Baudhāyana and Vasiṣṭha*, New Delhi: Motilal Banarsidass.

Epigraphic Sources

Bhandarkar, D.R. (1931–2). 'Mauryan Brāhmī Inscription of Mahāsthān', *Epigraphia Indica*, vol. XXI, pp. 83–91.

Hultzsch, E. (1991). *Corpus Inscriptionum Indicarum*, vol. I (Inscriptions of Aśoka), pp. 34–5.

Jayaswal, K.P. (1938). 'The Text of The Sohgaurah Plate', *Epigraphia Indica*, vol. XXII, pp. 1–3.

Mukherji, R. and S.K. Maity (1967). 'Mahāsthān Fragmentary Stone Plaque Inscription', *Corpus of Bengal Inscriptions Bearing on History and Civilization of Bengal*, Calcutta: Firma K.L.M., pp. 39–40.

Sircar, D.C. (1993). 'Mahāsthān Fragmentary Stone Plaque Inscription', *Select Inscriptions: Bearing on Indian History and Civilization*, vol. I, New Delhi: V.K. Publishing House (1st edn. 1942), pp. 79–80.

Secondary Sources

Ahmed, Bulbul and Md. Noorul Islam (2011). *The Mahasthan Hoard II of Silver Punch-marked Coins*, Dhaka: Asiatic Society of Bangladesh.

Alam, M.S. and J.F. Salles (eds.) (2001). *France-Bangladesh Joint Venture Excavations at Mahasthangarh: First Interim Report 1993-1999*, Dhaka: Department of Archaeology.

———(2017). *France-Bangladesh Joint Venture Excavations at Mahasthangarh: Second Interim Report 1993-1999*, Dhaka: Department of Archaeology.

Allchin, F.R., with contributions from G. Erdosy, R.E. Conningham, Dilip K. Chakrabarti and B. Allchin (1995). *The Archaeology of Early Historic South Asia, the Emergence of Cities and States*, Cambridge: Cambridge University Press.

Barua, B.M. (1930). 'The Sohgaura Copper-Plate Inscription', *Annals of the Bhandarkar Oriental Research Institute*, vol. 11, no. 1, Pune: Bhandarkar Oriental Research Institute, pp. 32–48.

———(1934). 'The Old Brahmī Inscription of Mahāsthān', *The Indian Historical Quarterly*, vol. X, pp. 57–66.

Basu Majumdar, S. (2018). 'Media of Exchange: Reflection on the Monetary History', *History of Bangladesh: Early Bengal in Regional Perspectives (up to c.1200 CE)*, vol. 2, ed. A.M. Chowdhury and R. Chakravarti, Dhaka: Asiatic Society of Bangladesh, pp. 233–68.

Basu Majumdar, S. and S. Bajpai (2014). *Select Early Historic Inscriptions: Epigraphic Perspectives on the Ancient Past of Chhattisgarh*, Raipur: Shatakshi Prakashan.

Basu Majumdar, S., S. Ghosh and S. Chatterjee (2020). 'Work Pattern Analysis at a Major Rock Edict Site: Kalsi', *Pratna Samiksha*, New Series, vol. 11, Kolkata: Centre for Archaeological Studies & Training, Eastern India, pp. 73–97.

Bhattacharyya, A. (1977). *Historical Geography of Ancient and Early Medieval Bengal*, Calcutta: Sanskrit Pustak Bhandar.

Bongard-Levin, G.M. (1958). 'Epigraphic Document of the Mauryas from Bengal', *Journal of the Asiatic Society, Letters*, vol. XXIV, no. 2, pp. 79–84.

Bongard-Levin, G.M. and A.A. Vigasin (1978–9). 'Society and State in Ancient India', in *IHR*, vol. 5, nos. 1–2, pp. 16–30.

Boussac, M.F. and M.S. Alam (2001). 'Coins', *France-Bangladesh Joint Venture Excavations at Mahasthangarh: First Interim Report 1993-1999*, ed. M.S. Alam and J.F. Salles, Dhaka: Department of Archaeology.

Briant, P. (1996). *Histoire de l'Empireperse: De Cyrus à Alexandre*, Paris: Fayard.

Bühler, G. (1896). 'The Sohgaura Copper Plate', *Indian Antiquary*, vol. XXV, p. 265.

Cameron, G.G. (1948). *Persepolis Treasury Tablets*, Chicago: The University of Chicago Press.

Chakravarti, R. (2016). *Exploring Early India up to c.AD 1300*, Delhi: Primus Books (3rd edn.).

Chakravarti, S.N. (1941). 'The Sohgaurah Copper-Plate Inscription', *Journal of the Royal Asiatic Society of Bengal. Letters*, vol. VII, no. 8, pp. 203–5.

Chattopadhyaya, B.D. (2003). *Studying Early India: Archaeology, Texts, and Historical Issues*, Delhi: Permanent Black.

———(2022). '"Autonomous space" and the authority of the state: the contradiction and its resolution in theory and practice in early India', *The Routledge Handbook of the State in Premodern India*, ed. H. Kulke and B.P. Sahu, London: Routledge, pp. 68–80.

Chowdhury, A.M. (2018). 'Early Bengal (up to *c*.3rd Century CE)', *History of Bangladesh: Early Bengal in Regional Perspectives (up to c.1200 CE)*, vol. 2, ed. A.M. Chowdhury and R. Chakravarti, Dhaka: Asiatic Society of Bangladesh, pp. 499–510.

Chowdhury, A.M. and M.S. Alam (2018). 'Historical Geography', *History of Bangladesh: Early Bengal in Regional Perspectives (up to c.1200 CE)*, vol. 1, ed. A.M. Chowdhury and R. Chakravarti, Dhaka: Asiatic Society of Bangladesh, pp. 1–34.

Chowdhury, A.M. and R. Chakravarti (eds.) (2018). *History of Bangladesh: Early Bengal in Regional Perspectives (up to c.1200 CE)*, vol. 1, Dhaka: Asiatic Society of Bangladesh.

Cunningham, A. (2000). *Reports from a Tour in Bihar and Bengal, 1879-1880. From Patna to Sonargaon*, vol. XV, Calcutta: Archaeological Survey of India (1st print 1882).

Fleet, J.F. (July 1907). 'The Inscription on the Sohgaura Plate', *The Journal of the Royal Asiatic Society of Great Britain and Ireland*, Cambridge: Cambridge University Press, pp. 509–32.

Ghosh, R. (2007). 'Re-Reading of The Sohgaurah Plaque Inscription by D.C. Sircar: A Note', *Journal of The Asiatic Society*, vol. XLIX, no. 4, pp. 110–13.

Ghosh, S. (2016). 'Re-reading Sohgaura Bronze Plaque Inscription: Situating it in Mauryan Context', *Studies in Indian Epigraphy*, vol. XLI, Mysore: The Epigraphical Society of India.

———(2018). 'The Sohgaura Bronze Plaque Inscription: A Critical Appraisal', *Recent Researches in Epigraphy and Numismatics*, ed. Mahesh Kalra and Suraj A. Pandit.

Grierson, G.A. (1907). 'The Sohgaura Inscription', *The Journal of the Royal Asiatic Society of Great Britain and Ireland*, Cambridge: Cambridge University Press, pp. 683–5.

Gupta, P.L. and T.R. Hardaker (1985). *Punch-marked Coinage of Indian Subcontinent: Magadha-Mauryan Series*, Nasik: IIRNS.

Habib, I. and V. Jha (2004). *Mauryan India*, vol. 4 of 'A People's History of India', New Delhi: Tulika Books.

Hossenakanda, M.K., et al. (2015). 'Alteration of the Alluvial Deposits of Wari-Bateshwar: Geoarchaeological Relevance of the Characterization of Grain Size and Clay Mineralogy', *Pratnatattva*, vol. 21, pp. 15–39.

Islam, S. (2018). 'Origin and Development of the Bangla Script', *History of Bangladesh: Early Bengal in Regional Perspectives (up to c.1200 CE)*, vol. II, ed. A.M. Chowdhury and R. Chakravarti, Dhaka: Asiatic Society of Bangladesh, pp. 607–22.

Mukherjee, B.M. (2000). *Coins and Currency Systems of Early Bengal (up to c. AD 300)*, Calcutta: Progressive Publishers.

Salles, J.F. (ed.) (2007). *Pundranagara, cité antique du Bengale: Fouilles de Mahasthan. Rapport préliminaire 1993–1999*, Brépols.

———(2015). *Mahasthan II, Fouilles du Rempart Est. Études archéologiques*, Brépols.

Sen, P.C. (1929). 'Mahasthan and Its Environs', *Varendra Research Society's Monographs*, no. 2, Rajshahi: Varendra Research Society.

Sircar, D.C. (1952). 'Notes on Some Inscriptions in The Collection of The Asiatic Society', *Journal of the Asiatic Society. Letters*. vol. XVIII, no. 1, pp. 1–3.

———(1966). *Indian Epigraphical Glossary*, New Delhi: Motilal Banarsidass.

———(2007). 'Notes on Some Inscriptions in The Collection of The Asiatic Society', *Journal of the Asiatic Society. Letters*. vol. XLIX, no. 4, pp. 101–3.

Smith, V.A. and A.F.R. Hoernle (1894). 'The Inscription of the Sohgaura Plate', *Proceedings of the Ancient Society of Bengal*, pp. 84–6.

Thapar, R. (1981). 'The State as Empire', *The Study of the State*, ed. H.J.M. Claessen and P. Skalnik, The Hague: Mouton Publishers, pp. 409–26.

———(1987). 'Towards the Definition of an Empire: The Mauryan State', *The Mauryas Revisited*, ed. R. Thapar, Calcutta: K.P. Bagchi, pp. 1–30.

———(2005). *History and Beyond: From Lineage to State*, New Delhi: Oxford India Paperbacks.

———(2013). *Readings in Early Indian History*, New Delhi: Oxford University Press.

———(2015). 'Towards the Definition of an Empire: The Mauryan State', *Interrogating Political Systems: Integrative Processes and States in Pre-Modern India*, ed. B.P. Sahu and H. Kulke, New Delhi: Manohar, pp. 141–71.

Further Readings

Basu Majumdar, S. (2016). *The Mauryas in Karnataka*, Kolkata: Mahabodhi Book Agency.

———(2017). 'State formation and religious processes in the north-south corridor of Chhattisgarh (from first century BC to eighth century AD)', *Studies in People's History*, vol. 4, issue 2, pp. 119–29.

Berliet, E. and B. Faticoni (2013). 'From the Mauryas to the Mughals. The Imperial History of Mahasthan', *Rivistadeglistudiorientali*, Nuova Serie, vol. 86, fasc. 1/4, Sapienza-Universita di Roma, pp. 25–46.

Bhattacharya, P.K. (2012). 'Irrigation and Agriculture in Ancient India' (Sectional President's Address), *Proceedings of the Indian History Congress*, vol. 73, Indian History Congress, pp. 18–34.

Biswas, Atreyi (1991). 'Storage and Rationing Facilities in Ancient India (from Earliest Times to the Early Christian Era)', *Proceedings of the Indian History Congress*, vol. 52, Indian History Congress, pp. 98–103.

Bühler, G. (1896). 'The Sohgaurā Copper Plate', *Wiener Zeitschriftfür die Kunde des Morgenlandes*, vol. 10, Vienna: Department of Oriental Studies, University of Vienna, pp. 138–48.

Fleet, J.F. (January 1908a). 'The Inscription on the Sohgaura Plate',

The Journal of the Royal Asiatic Society of Great Britain and Ireland, Cambridge: Cambridge University Press, pp. 187–8.

———(July 1908b). 'The Last Edict of Aśoka', *The Journal of the Royal Asiatic Society of Great Britain and Ireland*, Cambridge: Cambridge University Press, pp. 811–22.

———(July 1908c). 'The Inscription on the Sohgaura Plate', *The Journal of the Royal Asiatic Society of Great Britain and Ireland*, Cambridge: Cambridge University Press, pp. 822–3.

Fussman, G. (1987–8). 'Central and Provincial Administration in Ancient India: The Problem of the Maurya Empire', *Indian History Review*, vol. xiv, pp. 43–72.

Ghosh, R. (1996). 'Pundravardhana in the First Phase of Urbanization (4th Century BC–3rd Century AD)—A Study', *Proceedings of the Indian History Congress*, vol. 57, Indian History Congress, pp. 199–209.

Grierson, G.A. (1907). 'The Sohgaura Inscription', *The Journal of the Royal Asiatic Society of Great Britain and Ireland*, Cambridge: Cambridge University Press, pp. 683–5.

Habib, I. and F. Habib (1989). 'Mapping the Mauryan Empire', *Proceedings of the Indian History Congress*, vol. 50, Golden Jubilee Session, Indian History Congress, pp. 57–79.

Mishra, S.C. (2013). 'Some Reflections on the Loss of Learning and its Retrieval in the Wake of Twelve Years Drought', *Proceedings of the Indian History Congress*, vol. 74, Indian History Congress, pp. 154–61.

Parasher Sen, Aloka (1983). 'Assimilation Conservation and Expansion—Complex Strategies of Tribal Absorption in the Early Indian Context', *Proceedings of the Indian History Congress*, vol. 44, Indian History Congress, pp. 707–30.

Ray, H.P. (2006). 'The Archaeology of Bengal: Trading Networks, Cultural Identities', *Journal of the Economic and Social History of the Orient*, vol. 49, no. 1, Leiden: Brill, pp. 68–95.

Sahi, M.D.N. (1991). 'Jakhera – The Earliest Urban Centre of the Ganga Valley – An Evaluation of the Archaeological Evidence Obtained from the Site', *Proceedings of the Indian History Congress*, vol. 52, Indian History Congress, pp. 1010–18.

Salles, J.F. (2018). 'Mahasthan', *History of Bangladesh: Early Bengal in Regional Perspectives (up to c.1200 CE)*, vol. 2, ed A.M. Chowdhury and R. Chakravarti, Dhaka: Asiatic Society of Bangladesh, pp. 224–62.

Thaplyal, K.K. (2012). *Aśoka: The King and the Man*, New Delhi: Aryan Books International.

Tinti, P.G. (1996). 'On the Brāhmī Inscription of Mahāsthān', *Journal of Bengal Art*, vol. 1, ed. Enamul Haque, Dhaka: ICSBA, pp. 33–8.

Index

Achaemenid 61, 63
Ahmed, Nazimmudin 22
Alam, Shafiqul 22, 64
Arthaśāstra 53, 54, 74, 76, 82, 84, 97, 101
Āryaputra 96
Aśoka/Aśokan 31, 45, 48, 63, 76, 82, 89, 91, 93, 96, 101, 106, 107
āṭavikas 92
Atrai 19
autonomous spaces 90, 91, 94, 95

Bairagi Bhita 22
Bangarh 19, 25, 80
Bangladesh 19, 22, 48, 64, 79, 85, 102, 103, 104, 106
Batavyal 21
Beveridge, H. 20
Bhukti 20, 77
Bogra 19, 20, 21, 48
Buchanan-Hamilton, Francis 20

Chandraketugarh 78, 93
Chattopadhayaya, B.D. 26, 81, 85, 90, 95, 103
coinage 66, 67, 68, 69, 71, 93, 104
coins 32, 34, 36, 38, 40, 42, 56, 61, 63, 64, 65, 66, 67, 68, 69, 70, 71, 79, 83, 84, 93, 95, 102, 103, 104
core 26, 68, 91
Cunningham, Alexander 20

dagatiyāyika 33, 35, 36, 37, 39, 40, 43, 46, 73
Daiva 74
devānaṁpriya 89
Dhauli 89
Dikshit, K.N. 22
Dinajpur 20
dual control 94

elephants 90, 93, 94
emergency 32, 34, 36, 37, 38, 40, 42, 43, 44, 48, 51, 52, 53, 54, 55, 56, 57, 60, 73, 75, 76, 77, 83, 95

empire 25, 61, 65, 68, 76, 87, 88, 89, 90, 91, 92, 93, 94, 95, 97, 98, 99, 103, 105, 106
estampages 23
excavations 21, 22, 23, 26, 65, 81, 102, 103

flood 34, 36, 37, 38, 40, 42, 43, 44, 47, 61, 72, 73, 74, 80, 81, 86, 93, 98
fort/ fortification 21, 26, 60, 61, 62, 71, 81, 82

Gangaridae 94
Girnar 89
Govinda Bhita 22, 26
grains 38, 42, 43, 44, 50, 57, 58, 59, 60, 61, 62, 63, 65, 67, 69, 71, 75, 76, 78, 79, 82, 96
granary 32, 35, 36, 38, 41, 44, 50, 55, 57, 58, 59, 60, 61, 63, 65, 67, 69, 71, 78, 82, 83, 96, 98
Greeks 94

Indian Museum 23

Jambudvīpa 89
Jaugada 89

Kaliṅga 90
Kaliṅgan region 91
Karatoya 19, 25
kārṣāpaṇa 64, 66, 68, 69, 79, 94
Khodar Pathar Dhanp 21

Mahāmātra 32, 35, 39, 40, 42, 44, 56, 69, 71, 76, 77, 79, 82, 83, 88, 92, 95, 96, 97
Mahasthan 19, 20, 21, 22, 23, 24, 25, 26, 27, 28, 29, 30, 31, 33, 34, 35, 37, 39, 41, 43, 45, 46, 47, 48, 54, 55, 56, 57, 58, 59, 60, 61, 63, 64, 65, 66, 67, 68, 71, 73, 77, 78, 79, 80, 81, 82, 83, 84, 85, 88, 91, 92, 95, 96, 97, 98, 101, 102, 103, 104, 105, 106, 107
Major Rock Edict 76, 91, 102
Mañju 21
Mauryan 25, 31, 37, 52, 53, 54, 55, 63, 64, 65, 66, 67, 68, 69, 71, 81, 82, 83, 84, 85, 87, 88, 89, 90, 91, 92, 93, 94, 95, 96, 98, 99, 101, 104, 105, 106
medium of exchange 94, 95
metropolitan 44, 52, 54, 65, 68, 69, 79, 82, 84, 89, 90, 91, 92, 93, 94
money 42, 43, 56, 57, 58, 59, 61, 63, 64, 65, 67, 68, 69, 71, 76, 79, 81, 97, 98
Munir Ghoon 22

Nandi, K.C. 21

O' Donnell, Charles James 20

Pāṭaliputra 25, 79, 82, 84
Pauṇḍra/Pauṇḍras 19
periphery 90, 91
Persepolis 61, 62, 63, 68, 103
Punarbhava 19
Puṇḍranagara 19, 21, 25, 26, 32, 33, 34, 36, 37, 40, 42, 43, 44, 46, 56, 60, 71, 77, 78, 79, 81, 92
Puṇḍravardhana 20, 77

rājā Māgadhe 89
rampart enclosure 19

region/regions 19, 26, 44, 60, 64, 65, 67, 69, 71, 75, 76, 81, 85, 86, 89, 90, 91, 92, 93, 94, 95, 98, 99
regional 25, 42, 52, 64, 65, 76, 97, 102, 103, 104

Salles, Jean-Francois 22
Samāpā 90
Samvaṅgīya 39, 43, 44, 46, 47, 55, 56, 79, 86
Sannati 91
Sen, P.C. 20
Sohgaura 34, 48, 49, 52, 53, 54, 58, 59, 60, 73, 83, 85, 96, 101, 102, 103, 104, 105, 106, 116
Sohgaura bronze plaque 34, 48, 50, 61, 75, 96, 104
Southern territory 91
su-atyāyika/su-ātyāyika/su-atiyāyika 31, 33, 36, 38, 40, 43, 73, 77
sub-regions/sub-regional 19, 56, 66, 67, 69, 71, 72, 76, 79, 80, 84, 89, 92, 93, 94, 95, 96, 99
suka-tyāyika 38, 43

Tamralipta 93
Thapar, R. 89, 90, 91, 92, 105
Tosali 90
treasury 32, 35, 38, 40, 41, 42, 43, 47, 56, 58, 59, 61, 62, 63, 65, 67, 68, 69, 71, 73, 76, 79, 82, 89, 98, 103

urban centres 19, 20, 80, 83

Vaṅga 32, 44, 46, 56, 61, 64, 69, 71, 72, 80, 81, 83, 84, 85, 86, 88, 92, 95
Varendra 19, 21, 44, 56, 61, 67, 68, 83, 84, 88, 104

Wari Bateshwar 44, 69, 70, 80, 81, 104
Westmacott, E.V. 20

Colour Plates

FIG. 2.1: The Mahasthan record (front side or the incised side)

FIG. 2.2: The Mahasthan record (reverse side with fine polished)

FIG. 2.3 The Mahasthan record
showing the width of the stone

FIG. 2.4: The Mahasthan record
showing the polished ends and width of the stone

FIG. 2.5: The Mahasthan record from the side
showing the width of the stone

FIG. 2.6: Jogimara cave inscription, Chhattisgarh

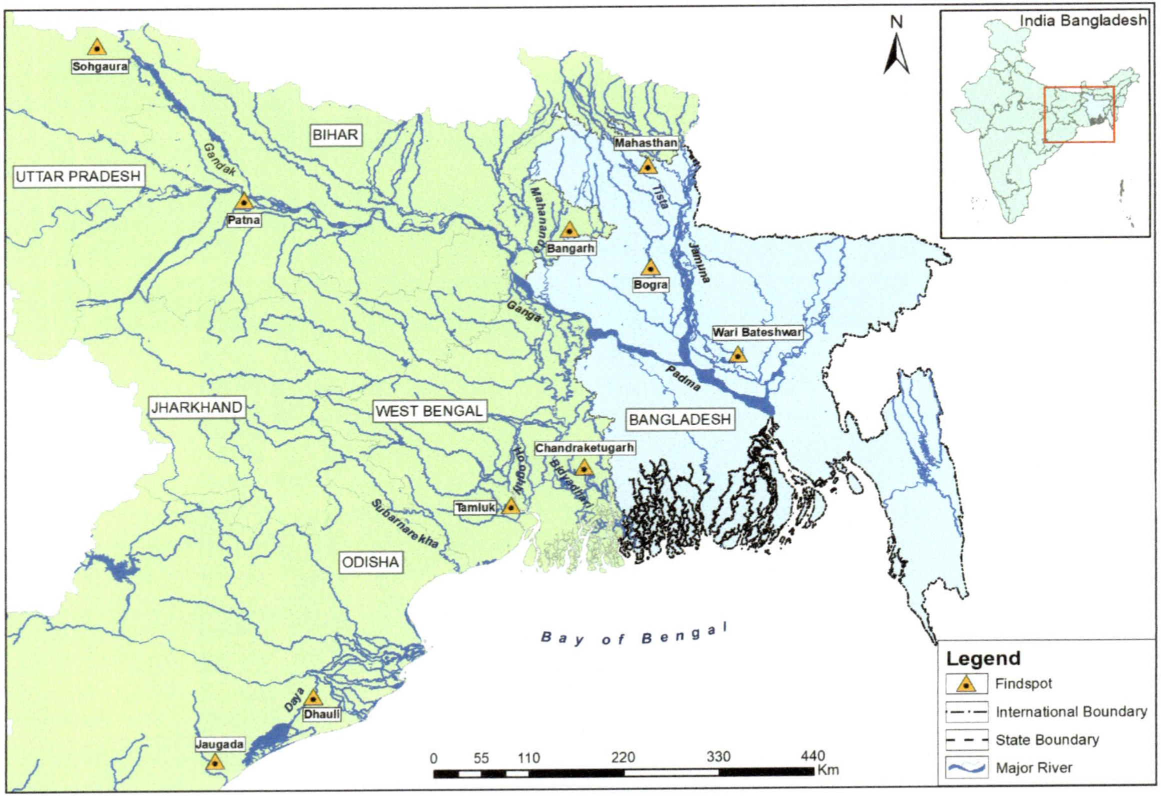

FIG. 3.1: Sohgaura and other important sites in Bengal and Odisha

Fig. 4.1: Imaginary reconstruction of the shape of the Mahasthan record